Playful Songs & Bible Stories

for Preschoolers

Group

Loveland, Colorado

Group's R.E.A.L. Guarantee to you:

This Group resource incorporates our R.E.A.L. approach to ministry—one that encourages long-term retention and life transformation. It's ministry that's:

Relational
Because learner-to-learner interaction enhances learning and builds Christian friendships.

Experiential
Because what learners experience through discussion and action sticks with them up to 9 times longer than what they simply hear or read.

Applicable
Because the aim of Christian education is to equip learners to be both hearers and doers of God's Word.

Learner-based
Because learners understand and retain more when the learning process takes into consideration how they learn best.

Playful Songs and Bible Stories for Preschoolers

Visit our Web site: **www.group.com**

Credits
Contributing Authors: Linda A. Anderson, Sharon Carey, Kim Cubberly, Ruthie Daniels, Lori Dunlap, Julie Lavender, Carol Mader, Barbie Murphy, Jennifer Nystrom, and Larry Shallenberger
Editor: Laurie Castañeda
Creative Development Editor: Karl Leuthauser
Chief Creative Officer: Joani Schultz
Copy Editor: Lyndsay E. Gerwing
Art Director: Kari K. Monson
Illustrators: Shelley Dieterichs, Joan Holub, Dana Regan, and Rebecca McKillip Thornburgh
Print Production Artist: Tracy K. Hindman
Cover Art Directors: Bambi Eitel and Ray Tollison
Cover Art Designers: Ray Tollison and Blukazoo Creative Studio
Cover Photographer: Daniel Treat
Production Manager: Peggy Naylor

Library of Congress Cataloging-in-Publication Data
Playful songs and Bible stories for preschoolers.
　　p. cm.
　Includes index.
　ISBN 0-7644-2534-X (pbk. : alk. paper)
　1. Christian education of preschool children. 2. Sunday schools--Hymns.
　3. Bible stories, English. 4. Finger play. I. Group Publishing.
BV1475.8.P58 2003
268'.432--dc21
　　　　　　　　　　　　　　　　　　　　　　2002156755

10 9 8 7 6 5　　　　12 11 10 09 08 07
Printed in the United States of America.

Contents

Joshua to the Judges

Israel's Kings

Elijah and Elisha

The Prophets

Jesus Is Born

Jesus' Ministry Begins

Jesus' Miracles

Jesus' Teachings

Jesus Dies for Our Sins

The Beginnings of the Church

Introduction

What are some of the special songs you learned as a young child? Maybe your mother hummed "Twinkle, Twinkle, Little Star" before you went to sleep every night. Perhaps you remember hammering out "Mary Had a Little Lamb" on the piano. Isn't it amazing that you can still sing all the words to the songs you learned years ago?

Music cements words and ideas into our memories. A simple melody provides powerful learning hooks and memory triggers that help us remember words and concepts for our entire lives. From the time children begin to speak, they repeat simple, repetitive tunes. *Playful Songs and Bible Stories for Preschoolers* uses the power of simple melodies and music to help children learn, remember, and love God's Word.

A parent recently shared how amazed he was when he heard his five-year-old singing "Jesus Loves Me" at the top of his lungs as he was swinging in their back yard the previous week. Conscious of the sound his son's voice produced as it echoed across the valley their home overlooked, the dad ventured outside and asked his son if he would sing a little more quietly so he wouldn't disturb the neighbors. To his surprise, his son replied, "But, Dad, my teacher told me we should tell everyone about Jesus, so I'm telling everyone that Jesus loves them." Amazed and embarrassed, he encouraged his son to continue singing.

Playful Songs and Bible Stories for Preschoolers provides simple songs for the seventy-five most important Bible stories. But music is just the beginning! Every Bible story provides a finger play for children to learn the story as they move their bodies. Interactive Bible stories give the details and heart of each Bible story as you read the stories and lead children in responding and reacting.

During some of the Bible stories in the book, food is used both as a prop and later as the snack. Be aware that some children have food allergies that can be dangerous. Know your children, and consult with parents about allergies their children may have. Also be sure to read food labels carefully as hidden ingredients can cause allergy-related problems.

Use this resource to supplement your existing curriculum or as the essential component of your Bible lesson. Used in concert, the songs, finger plays, and interactive Bible stories will teach and reinforce Bible learning while delighting your preschool children. Most important, children will remember the Bible songs and stories for the rest of their lives!

God Made the World

This Is the Way God Made the World

Sing "This Is the Way God Made the World" to the tune of "The Mulberry Bush."

This is the way God made the world (*form a circle above head with both hands and sway to the rhythm*),
Made the world, made the world.
This is the way God made the world—
The land, the sky, the sea.

God put the moon up in the sky (*shield eyes with hand and look up*),
In the sky, in the sky.
God put the moon up in the sky.
The moon is way up high.

The sun is shining big and bright (*open and close hands, with palms facing outward*),
Big and bright, big and bright.
The sun is shining big and bright.
God's sun gives us light.

The trees are moving in the breeze (*hold arms up like branches and sway back and forth*),
In the breeze, in the breeze.
The trees are moving in the breeze.
God made the big, tall trees.

The flowers are growing big and tall (*pretend to be small, then "grow up" slowly like a flower*),
Big and tall, big and tall.
The flowers are growing big and tall.
God's flowers are for us all.

This is the way God made the world (*form a circle above head with both hands and sway to the rhythm*),
Made the world, made the world.
This is the way God made the world—
The land, the sky, the sea.

All in Seven Days

Lots happened in just seven days—the entire universe was created. Your children may not grasp the magnitude of all God made, but they can begin to understand that God did it all in seven days.

On day one (*hold up one finger*),

God made dark (*cover eyes*) **and light.** (*Uncover eyes.*)

On day two (*hold up two fingers*),

God made the sky. (*Point up.*)

On day three (*hold up three fingers*),

God made land and plants. (*Hold one arm out in front of you. Brush over the top with the other hand, then raise arm up and wiggle fingers.*)

On day four (*hold up four fingers*),

God made the sun and stars. (*Form a large circle with arms over head and then hold both arms up and wiggle fingers.*)

On day five (*hold up five fingers*),

God made birds and fish. (*Flap arms, then put hands together pointing away and wiggle hands.*)

On day six (*hold up six fingers*),

God made animals and people. (*Hold hands up in back of head like bunny ears, then hug yourself.*)

On day seven (*hold up seven fingers*),

God's all done. He made it all (*with palms up, spread hands out*)

In just seven days. (*Hold up seven fingers.*)

God Made the World

Genesis 1–2

Bible Point: God created everything.

Begin by teaching your children the following "Creation chant" and having them hold up the correct number of fingers as you count.

One, two, three, four, five, six, seven. (*Hold up the correct number of fingers as you count.*)

God created earth and heaven. (*Point up to the sky with both hands.*)

Say: **One! The very first day ever, there was nothing—no people, animals, grass, or stars. But God was there, and God wanted to make something wonderful. First God made light. He put the light in one place and the dark in another. He called the light "day" and the darkness "night." And that was the very first day. One!**

Repeat the seven day chant. Hold up two fingers.

Say: **Two! The next day, God made water. God put the water together in separate places with a space in between that he called "sky." That was the second day. Two!**

Repeat the chant. Hold up three fingers.

Say: **Three! Next, God made dry land. The water made lakes, oceans, and rivers, and left dry land. Next God made plants—grass, trees, vegetables, fruits, and flowers. It looked beautiful. That was the third day. Three!**

Repeat the chant. Hold up four fingers.

Say: **Four! Now God made the sun, the moon, and the stars up in the sky. Four!**

Repeat the chant. Hold up five fingers.

Say: **Five! So far, everything God made was very quiet. But now God made birds and fish. Now there were sweet songs and splashing sounds. Five!**

Repeat the chant. Hold up six fingers.

Say: **Six! Next God made animals—elephants and ants, leopards and turtles. And best of all—people! God made the first man and woman, Adam and Eve. Six!**

Repeat the chant. Hold up seven fingers.

Say: **Seven! Then everything was done, and God just stopped to enjoy all he had made. He rested. Day seven!**

Ask: • **How many days did God take to create our beautiful world?**

• **What do you like best that God created?**

• **What would you like to thank God for creating?**

Say: **God created everything! Let's show him how thankful we are for creating our beautiful world and all the things in it.** Let the children take turns spontaneously thanking God for the things they like—for example, "Thank you, God, for making monkeys."

God Made People

God Made You; God Made Me

Sing "God Made You; God Made Me" to the tune of "This Old Man."

God made you; God made me. (*Point to a friend, then point to yourself.*)
God made each one differently,
But we're all part of one big family. (*Hold up one finger.*)
God made each one differently. (*Point to others.*)

God made you; God made me. (*Point to a friend, then point to yourself.*)
God made everyone we see,
But we're all part of one big family. (*Hold up one finger.*)
God made everyone we see. (*Point to others.*)

God Made People

Help your children understand how special they are to God by teaching them this finger play about how God created the first man and woman.

God would make man in a special way.
He bent down and scooped up some clay. (*Pretend to scoop with one hand.*)

He shaped it just right and blew life into the man. (*Blow into open palm.*)

Adam was the beginning of God's "people plan."
But God knew that Adam needed a wife (*hold up one index finger*),

Someone to love him and share his life. (*Hug yourself.*)

So God took a rib from Adam's side
And then made Eve, Adam's new bride. (*Hold up one index finger, then the other.*)

God makes each of us with special care—
In your town, my town, and everywhere.
(*Point to a friend, point to yourself, then point to everyone.*)

God Made People

Genesis 1:26-31; 2:4-25

Bible Point: God created you and loves you.

Man was God's final and best creation! Everything else was *spoken* into existence, but man was *formed* by God's hand in his image and given God's own breath of life. Each person is of great value to God. As you tell this Bible story of how God loved Adam and Eve, emphasize God's love for each of your children. You will be creating a foundation of love and security that will continue to develop in your children's hearts as they hear and experience more about God's love.

Before you begin, tell the children that they will get to do motions to help them understand the Bible story. Instruct them to do the same motions that you do during the Bible story.

Say: **God made the sun, moon, and stars; and he made the earth to be the perfect home for people. There was water in rivers, lakes, and oceans.** Make waving motions with your hands. **There were plants for shade and good fruits to eat.** Touch hands above your head, then pretend to pick an apple and eat it. **There were birds singing.** Flap your arms. **And there were lots of animals. Let's all make our favorite animal sounds.** Have kids make animal sounds. **But there was no one for God to love and talk with.**

Ask: • **How do you feel when you don't have anyone to play with?**

Say: **So God made a person—someone he could love and talk with. He scooped up some dirt and shaped it into a man.** Pretend to scoop dirt and form it into something. **God blew his own breath into the man's body.** Blow onto your pretend image. **Show me how you can blow your breath.** Encourage kids to blow into their cupped hands. **That's how Adam, the very first man, became alive! The Bible says God breathed into him the breath of life!**

God made a beautiful garden for Adam to live in. It had a river in it and lots of wonderful plants. God even let Adam name all the animals!

Ask: • **Have you ever gotten to name a pet?**

• **What did you name it?**

Say: **So all the animals came to Adam, and he decided what to call them. This one he called a bear.** Have children growl like bears. **This one he called a bee.** Have children buzz like bees. **Here was one he called a cow.** Have kids make mooing sounds.

Ask: • **What other animals do you think Adam named?** Have children say the names of more animals and make their sounds.

Say: **Adam saw that all the animals had partners except for him. Adam was lonely, so God made Adam a partner—a woman to be Adam's wife.**

First he made Adam go to sleep. Have kids place their heads on their hands and make snoring noises. **While Adam was sleeping, God took a rib from Adam's side.** Have kids stop snoring. Show children where their ribs are, and let them feel one of their ribs. **God used one of Adam's ribs and created the first woman. When Adam woke up and saw her, he was very happy. Adam got to give her a name also.**

Ask: • **What name would you give a new girl?**

• **What do you think Adam named his new friend from God?**

Say: **He named her "Eve," which means "life." She was exactly what he wanted. God had created a special partner for Adam.**

The world was perfect! God had friends—Adam and Eve—to love and care for, and Adam had a friend—Eve—to love and care for. That was the day God made people.

Have the children stand in a circle.

Say: **The day God made you, he must have been just as excited to breathe his breath of life into your body as he was with Adam.** Have the children hold hands and blow toward each other. **You are as special to God. He created you, and he loves you always!** Have children come close together and form a large classroom hug.

Adam and Eve Sin

Silly Adam

Sing "Silly Adam" to the tune of "Allouette."

Silly Adam, silly, silly Adam. *(Roll eyes and make a silly face.)*

Silly Adam, you can't hide from God. *(Cover eyes with hands.)*

You can't hide behind a tree *(put arms up and wiggle fingers),*

Even if you're on your knees! *(Touch your knees.)*

On your back! *(Touch a friend's back.)*

In a sack! *(Cover your eyes.)*

Ohhhhhh!

(Repeat chorus.)

Leaving the Garden

This simple review of the Bible story will help your children remember that God loves us even when we disobey.

God created a beautiful world
Where he could walk and talk with Adam and
Eve. *(Walk fingers up arm.)*

He said, "Eat all you want, except from one tree.
(Hold hand to mouth, then hold up index finger.)

Don't even stop to look or see." *(Wag finger back and forth.)*

But along came a snake *(wiggle index finger horizontally)*

That told Eve a lie. *(Make a sad face.)*

He said, "God would never let you die."
Eve ate the fruit, and Adam did too *(hold hand to mouth, then move hand away from mouth),*

So God had to close their garden new. *(Bring palms together in a clap.)*

Adam and Eve Sin

Genesis 3

Bible Point: God forgives us when we disobey.

Even at this tender age, your children know that it's wrong to disobey. However, like Eve, their choice to obey is often blinded by the physical view of what they want. As you ask questions such as "What could happen if you took your friend's toy, if you hit your brother, or if you chose to obey?" you help your children learn to obey as well as begin their development into abstract thinking.

Before you begin, have children practice shouting, "Yeah!" when you give a thumbs up and "Boo!" when you show a thumbs down. Tell children to watch for these signs throughout the Bible story.

Say: **Long, long ago, when God had first made the world, he made a special place for Adam and Eve to live. It was a beautiful garden with rivers, flowers, and lots of fruit to eat.** Show thumbs up, and have kids shout, "Yeah!" **Adam and Eve got to spend time walking and talking with God.** Show thumbs up, and have kids shout, "Yeah!"

Adam and Eve loved living in their beautiful garden! God asked them to obey only one rule: Eat all the fruit you want, but don't even touch the fruit from the tree in the center of the garden. God had told Adam and Eve that if they ate the fruit of that tree, they would die. Show thumbs down, and have kids shout, "Boo!" **Adam and Eve were very good about obeying God.** Show thumbs up, and have kids shout, "Yeah!"

But that changed when a mean, snakelike creature tried to trick Eve by telling her lies. Show thumbs down, and have kids shout, "Boo!" **The creature told Eve if she ate fruit from the tree in the center of the garden, she'd become as smart as God. Eve looked at the fruit on that tree again and thought about it. She thought about disobeying God.** Show thumbs down, and have kids shout, "Boo!"

The fruit looked and smelled good. Eve looked at the fruit and wanted to touch and eat it.

Ask: • **What do you think will happen if Eve picks and eats the fruit?**

• **What do you think Eve should do? Why?**

Say: **She picked the fruit and ate it.** Show thumbs down, and have kids shout, "Boo!" **She went to find Adam to give him some.**

Ask: • **Do you think Adam will eat the fruit? Why?**

Say: **Eve found Adam and gave him some fruit. He ate it too.** Show thumbs down, and have kids shout, "Boo!" **Adam and Eve knew they weren't supposed to eat that fruit, but they did it anyway.**

Ask: • **Have you ever done something you weren't supposed to do? What happened?**

• **Did you want anyone to know what you did?**

• **How did you feel when someone found out?**

Say: **Soon God came looking for Adam and Eve in the garden. But Adam and Eve didn't want God to see them because they knew they had disobeyed him.** Show thumbs down, and have kids shout, "Boo!" **They felt awful inside—maybe even sick to their stomachs. God already knew what they had done, but God loved them and looked for them anyway.** Show thumbs up, and have kids shout, "Yeah!" **He was very sad because they disobeyed his one and only rule. Now God had to show them the consequences for disobeying.**

Because Adam and Eve had disobeyed God, they had to leave the beautiful garden. They had to go to a place where they had to grow their own garden and plant their own fruit trees. Adam and Eve were never allowed to go back to the beautiful garden again.

God was sad. Adam and Eve hurt God when they disobeyed, but God never stopped loving them. God provides forgiveness for all of us. Show thumbs up, and have kids shout, "Yeah!" **We may have consequences like timeouts when we disobey, but God still loves us.** Show thumbs up, and have kids shout, "Yeah!" **Adam and Eve had to leave their beautiful garden home and weren't allowed to live forever anymore, but God loved them and forgave them.** Show thumbs up, and have kids shout, "Yeah!"

God forgives us when we disobey. God loves us so much that he sent his Son, Jesus, to live here in our world and die for our sins. When we ask God to forgive us for disobeying, he remembers that Jesus died for our sins and forgives us. We don't have to hide from God, like Adam and Eve did, because God loves us and has already forgiven us! Show thumbs up, and have kids shout, "Yeah!"

Noah Builds an Ark

The Lord Will Keep His Promises

Sing "The Lord Will Keep His Promises" to the tune of "The Muffin Man."

The Lord will keep his promises, promises, promises. *(Wave arms over head.)*
The Lord will keep his promises.
God never tells a lie. *(Show thumbs up with both thumbs.)*

Noah obeyed and built the ark, built the ark, built the ark. *(Pretend to build, pounding fist over fist.)*
Noah obeyed and built the ark.
God never tells a lie. *(Show thumbs up with both thumbs.)*

Animals on the ark came two by two, two by two, two by two. *(Hold up two fingers on each hand, placing them one in front of the other repeatedly.)*
Animals on the ark came two by two.
God never tells a lie. *(Show thumbs up with both thumbs.)*

God shut the door when the rain came down, rain came down, rain came down. *(Make one loud clap.)*
God shut the door when the rain came down.
God never tells a lie. *(Show thumbs up with both thumbs.)*

It rained and poured for forty days, forty days, forty days. *(Wiggle fingers downward.)*
It rained and poured for forty days.
God never tells a lie. *(Show thumbs up with both thumbs.)*

The boat hit land when the water dried, water dried, water dried. *(Take a small leap.)*
The boat hit land when the water dried.
God never tells a lie. *(Show thumbs up with both thumbs.)*

The Lord will keep his promises, promises, promises. *(Wave arms over head.)*
The Lord will keep his promises.
God never tells a lie. *(Show thumbs up with both thumbs.)*

Do What God Says

Standing for God and what he says to do can be a tall order, especially for young children. This finger play emphasizes how Noah stood tall for God.

God told Noah to build a big boat. *(Make both hands into fists and pound on top of each other.)*

No one believed that it would float! *(Wag finger back and forth.)*

But Noah did what God said. *(Place hand behind ear and lean as if listening.)*

Build it tall. *(Lift hands above head.)*

Build it wide. *(Spread arms wide.)*

Build it strong so all can hide. *(Show strong arms.)*

No one believed that it would float! (*Wag finger back and forth.*)

But Noah did what God said. (*Place hand behind ear and lean as if listening.*)

Noah Builds an Ark

Genesis 6:5-22

Bible Point: We can choose to obey God.

Noah lived during a wicked time, but he still lived God's way. What a challenging situation! But is ours so different today? We live God's way in a world that is trying to do things its own way. You can encourage your children to live differently from those around them through the example of Noah.

Before you begin, teach your children to say, "Noah did it God's way," each time you point to them as indicated in the story.

Say: **This story happened long ago when people everywhere were very mean. They hurt each other. They stole from each other. No one except Noah obeyed God.** Point to children to respond, "Noah did it God's way."

Noah kept telling the people to turn to God because the earth was going to be destroyed. But nobody listened. They just laughed. God told Noah that he was going to destroy the earth—all except Noah and his family. Point to children to respond, "Noah did it God's way."

God told Noah to build a big boat out of wood from the cypress tree. Noah could have used wood from an oak tree or a cherry tree or a pine tree, but... (point to children to respond, "Noah did it God's way") **Noah used cypress wood.**

God told Noah to build it 450 feet long and 75 feet wide and 45 feet high with three decks and rooms in it. Noah could have made a smaller boat with only two decks, or he could have made it bigger with five decks, but... (point to children to respond, "Noah did it God's way").

God told Noah to cover the boat with pitch inside and out and to put a big door in the side of it. Noah could have said, "Forget the pitch. It is too hard to do." He could have put the door in the top. But... (point to children to respond, "Noah did it God's way").

God said to Noah that he was to take two of lots of animals—two birds, two bugs of each type, two buffaloes, two bears, and even two of every kind of butterfly! And God wanted Noah to take all kinds of food for him, his family, and all the animals into the big boat too. Noah could have said, "I don't like bears, so no bears on my boat." Or he could have said, "That is too much work to do to get all that food." But... (point to children to respond, "Noah did it God's way").

Yes, Noah could have chosen to do things his own way. But... (point to children to respond, "Noah did it God's way"). **We all have choices too. Will you do things your way? Or will you be like Noah and** (have the children say this with you) **"do it God's way"?**

Ask: • **How did Noah obey God?**

• **When are some times you've chosen to obey your parents? What happened?**

• **How can you obey God this week?**

Say: **Obeying our parents is one way we obey God each day. When you have a choice to do the right thing or something you know is wrong, remember that Noah chose to do the right things. Noah chose to obey God. We can choose to obey God too.**

The Animals Climb Aboard

All Aboard!

Sing "All Aboard!" to the tune of "This Old Man."

Two by two, two by two (hold up two fingers),
Look—here comes a walking zoo! (Look around.)
Hear the STOMP, STOMP (stomp feet),
Flitter-flitter flip!
All aboard on Noah's ship! (Motion with arm to come on.)

In we go (march in place),
Nice and slow,
Careful not to step on toes! (Lift foot back.)
Hear the STOMP, STOMP (stomp feet),
Flitter-flitter flip!
All aboard on Noah's ship! (Motion with arm to come on.)

Safe in the Boat

This finger play will help children remember that God kept Noah and the animals safe in the ark.

Here is Noah (hold up pointer finger on one hand)

And the boat Noah built. (Cup hand under finger.)

Just as God told him. (Point up to God.)

Here come the animals, two by two. (Bounce both hands, each holding up two fingers.)

Here come the _____. (Have children name an animal and make the sound of that animal. Continue this as many times as you would like.)
God shut the door of the ark. (Make a loud clap.)

God sent the rain, drop by drop. (Tap fingers on legs.)

God sent harder rain. (Pat hands softly on legs.)

Now it is a downpour. (Hit hands harder and faster on legs.)

But Noah and the animals were safe on the ark. (Cup hands in front of body.)

The Animals Climb Aboard

Genesis 7:1-16

Bible Point: God protects us.

Can you imagine the scene? Artists for hundreds of years have tried to picture it. The ark is finished, and animals of every sort, from near and far, familiar and bizarre, start arriving. What chaos! What noise! What color! And what an amazing God! How could Noah's neighbors not have wondered in amazement at what was happening? Enjoy talking with your children about all the types of animals God sent into the ark, how God protected them all, and how God provides ways of protection for the children each day.

Before you begin, distribute sheets of colored construction paper—white, red, black, brown, blue, green, yellow, and gray—to the children. Call out the names of the colors a few times before you start the story to make sure children can identify the names of the colors they are holding. Each time you come to a color word in the story, pause for the children who have that color to hold up their papers.

Say: **Noah was a man who lived long ago and loved God very much. God had told Noah to build a big boat called an "ark." Noah obeyed and did it. It took Noah a long time—years and years and years! But finally the big *brown* boat was finished!** Have children hold up the brown papers. **Noah wondered what to do next. But he didn't wonder for very long.**

Soon Noah saw animals of all colors coming to the ark. He saw big animals and little animals. Noah saw rosy *red* foxes. Have children hold up the red papers. **He saw flying birds and crawling bugs. Noah saw big *black* bears.** Have the children hold up the black papers. **He saw slow-moving turtles and racing cheetahs. Noah saw glittery *green* alligators.** Have the children hold up the green papers. **He saw animals he knew, like dogs, and animals he had never even imagined, maybe kangaroos and aardvarks. Noah saw whispery soft *white* doves.** Have the children hold up the white papers. **The animals kept coming two by two until the ark was completely full.**

There were animals everywhere! But there was just enough room for everything and everyone. God had planned everything out perfectly. He had told Noah to build the ark just the right size so all the animals would fit. God's plans are always right.

Noah looked up and saw big *gray* clouds starting to form in the sky. Have the children hold up the gray papers. **Bright flashes of *yellow* lightning ran across the sky.** Have the children hold up the yellow papers. **Then big drops of *blue* rain began to fall.** Have the

children hold up the blue papers.

Noah and his family were all aboard. Two of all the animals were aboard. Now it was time for the next part of God's plan. Because everyone was safely aboard, God himself shut the big *brown* door on the side of the ark. Have the children hold up the brown papers.

God had a wonderful plan for saving Noah and all the animals. And God has wonderful plans for you, too. You are an important part of God's big *colorful* plan. Have all the children stand and shake their papers.

Ask: • **How did God protect Noah and his family during the flood?**

• **How has God protected you and your family?**

• **How can you thank him for protecting you?**

Say: **God promised to protect Noah, his family, and all the animals God placed on the ark. Just as God protected Noah and his family, God protects us every day, even when we can't see it.**

Tip From the Trenches

If you have a small group of children, you may need to have some children hold two colors of paper. Cut the papers in half for the children to be able to hold two pieces more easily. This will get confusing, however, for younger preschoolers. If possible, give children four years old and older two sheets.

The Boat Begins to Float

The Ark Song

Sing "The Ark Song" to the tune of "Row, Row, Row Your Boat."

Sail, sail, sail the ark (*make wavelike motions with hands*)
On the waves at sea.
Up and down and all around (*stand on tiptoe, then bend low and turn around*)—
God takes care of me.

Sail, sail, sail the ark (*make wavelike motions with hands*);
It's like a floating bus.
Monkeys, zebras, kangaroos (*act like an animal of your choice*)—
God takes care of us.

Everything Covered With Water

Before beginning this finger play, point out that while everything else in the whole world was covered with water, Noah, his family, and the animals were safe on the ark.

Watch the raindrops, falling down. (*Hold hands out and wiggle fingers while moving hands down.*)

More and more rain. (*Wiggle fingers and bring hands down faster.*)
It falls on the trees. (*Cup hand and place index finger of opposite hand inside.*)

It falls on the mountains. (*Put fingertips of both hands together to form a peak above head.*)

It falls on the boat with Noah and the animals. (*Make an animal sound.*)
The water goes up and up and up. (*Lift hands slowly until above head.*)

It covers the trees. (*Cup hand and place index finger of opposite hand inside.*)

It covers the mountains. (*Put fingertips of both hands together to form a peak above head.*)

But it doesn't cover Noah and the animals. (*Wag finger.*)

His big boat is safe, safe, safe! (*Hug yourself.*)

The Boat Begins to Float

Genesis 7:17–8:5

Bible Point: We can trust God.

Six long months crowded onto a boat with an unimaginable number of animals. The smells alone must have been enough to make everyone want to jump overboard! But there was nowhere else to go. This was a time of really trusting God that the floodwaters would recede and that life would start over. This story should encourage your children to keep going until God shows them the next step to take.

Each time you see a motion in italics, have your children do that motion with you. The more dramatic you are, the more children enthusiastically participate.

Say: **Everyone was on the ark—Noah, his wife, his three sons and their wives, and all the animals from around the world. It was crowded, it was noisy, and it was smelly! The rains started falling very hard. The boat started to move. Soon the boat was *rocking side to side*.** Have kids rock side to side. **The boat *rocked back and forth*.** Have kids rock back and forth. **And still it rained! The waters *rose higher and higher*.** Have kids place their hands in front of them and then raise their hands slowly. **The water now covered all the trees. Everything was underwater. Even the *tall mountains*** (have kids bring the tips of the fingers of both hands together to form a peak) **were underwater. The rain went on for *forty days*.** Have kids hold up ten fingers spread apart and then close them and open them three more times to total forty. **Then the rain stopped.**

The boat *rocked back and forth*. Have kids rock back and forth. **The boat *rocked side to side*.** Have kids rock side to side. **Days and days and months and months went by. Noah wondered what would happen. Everyone on the boat wondered what would happen. But they knew that God was going to make everything OK. They waited for God to show them what to do next.** Place your index finger on your lips, and have the children wait quietly for about fifteen seconds.

God sent a wind to *blow on the water*. Have kids blow. **The water went slowly *down, down, down*.** Have kids hold hands way up above their heads with palms facing down and then slowly lower them. **The ark stopped with a bump. Now everyone on the ark knew that God had taken away the floodwaters. All were safe and sound during their travels over the water.**

Ask: • **What happened after God closed the door to the ark?**

• **How do you think Noah and his family felt inside the ark?**

• **How would you feel if you were on a boat for such a long time and could finally get off?**

Say: **Noah and his family trusted God when they were building the ark. They trusted God when they packed the ark with all the supplies they needed. They trusted God when all the animals came onto the ark. And they trusted God when he closed the door and all the rain began to fall. When you feel like you're having a bad day, remember that you can trust God and he will make it OK.**

God Paints a Rainbow

The Rainbow Song

Give each of the children a different color streamer about three feet long to sway with during the song. Sing "The Rainbow Song" to the tune of "Did You Ever See a Lassie?"

Did you ever see a rainbow, a rainbow, a rainbow? *(Raise arms in a circle above head and sway.)*
Did you ever see a rainbow way up in the sky?
With yellow and orange and purple and blue—
Oh, God made the rainbow for me and for you.
(Make a circle above head, then point to yourself and then to someone else.)

Did you ever see a rainbow, a rainbow, a rainbow? *(Raise arms in a circle above head and sway.)*
Did you ever see a rainbow way up in the sky?
With red and yellow and orange and green—
Oh, God made the rainbow for you and for me.
(Make a circle above head, then point to someone else and then to yourself.)

God's Promise

Children enjoy seeing rainbows. You can help them remember who sends the rainbows with this finger play.

See the waves a-rocking. *(Make wave motions.)*

Down went the waters as the rain was stopping. *(Slowly make smaller waves, then stop.)*
God said it was time to leave the big boat.
(Point away.)

No longer did it have to float.
God painted a rainbow in the sky. *(Sweep hands over head.)*

God kept Noah and his family safe and dry.

God Paints a Rainbow

Genesis 8:6–9:17

Bible Point: God loves us and doesn't forget about us.

Dry ground at last! After such a long time, God sent reassurance of his love and faithfulness. He spread a rainbow across the sky to remind us even today that he has not forgotten us or his promises to us. Use this story as a way of teaching your children to remember God's love each time they see a rainbow.

This is a rhyming story with the last word of the couplet left out. Most preschoolers will be able to guess the rhyming word with a little emphasis on the italicized word in the first line and will want to repeat the story again.

Noah and the animals were on the ark many *days*.
The ark finally stopped on a mountain, where it [stays].

Noah needed dry land to be *found*.
So he sent out a dove to search all [around].

But the dove came back—she found no dry place to *rest*.
Noah waited, then sent her back out for another quick [test].

This time she came back with a leaf in her *beak*,
But Noah waited still longer, another whole [week].

Out went the dove, but she didn't come *back*.
God told Noah, "It's time to [unpack]."

So Noah, his family, and the animals went *out*.
They stopped to give thanks to God with a [shout]!
And God said to Noah, "I want you to *know*,

I make you a promise—here's a beautiful [rainbow].

This rainbow's a sign that I mean what I *say*.
I'll never destroy the world again in this [way]."
Noah knew God loved them. The promise is *true*.
When you see a rainbow, you can remember that God loves [you].

Ask: • **How did God show Noah that he loved him?**
• **When was God with Noah and his family?**
• **When is God with you and your family?**
Say: **Sometimes others might forget about us, but God never does. Just as God was always with Noah and his family, God loves us and doesn't forget about us either.**

If your class has trouble guessing the missing words, read the story through a couple of times, emphasizing the missing words. Then try it again, leaving off the words.

The People Build a Tower

Jesus Loves Me

Your children will enjoy singing this familiar tune in different languages. Practice first without the CD, then just let the children do the motions and sing the words they remember.

Jesus (*touch middle fingers to palms of opposite hands one at a time*)
Loves me! (*Hug yourself.*)
This I know (*point to head*),
For the Bible tells me so (*place hands together like an open book*);
Little ones (*pat the air as if touching children's heads*)
To him belong (*point up*),
They are weak (*drop arms and shoulders down and look weak*)
But he is strong. (*Show strong arms.*)

Chorus in English:
Yes, Jesus (*touch middle fingers to palms of opposite hands one at a time*)
Loves me! (*Hug yourself.*)
Yes, Jesus loves me!
Yes, Jesus loves me!
The Bible tells me so. (*Place hands together like an open book.*)

Chorus in Spanish:
Sí, Jesús me ama!
Sí, Jesús me ama!
Sí, Jesús me ama!
La Biblia me dice así.

Chorus in French:
Oui, Jésus m'aime!
Oui, Jésus m'aime!
Oui, Jésus m'aime!
La Bible m'indique ainsi.

Chorus in German:
Ja Jesus liebt mich!
Ja Jesus liebt mich!
Ja Jesus liebt mich!
Die Bibel sagt mir so.

Chorus in Italian:
Sì, Gesú mi ama!
Sì, Gesú mi ama!
Sì, Gesú mi ama!
La Bibbia mi dice così.

They Built It Tall

This little finger play will help your children remember the main ideas of the story of the Tower of Babel.

Brick by brick, they built it high (*alternate pounding one fist on top of the other*)—

A mighty tower to the sky. (*Continue pounding and moving up.*)
They all spoke the same
And understood each one's name. (*Touch side of head, then point to others.*)

They all chose to live together. (*Hug yourself.*)

And they didn't care whether
God said stay or told them to go. (*Point finger down, then point away.*)

But God said, "No. (*Wag finger back and forth.*)

No tower, no same talk.
Gather and go on a faraway walk." *(Point away.)*

They looked for others who spoke just like
them *(point to others)*

And settled down in the places God originally
planned. *(Make praying hands.)*

Tip From the Trenches

Some children may never have been exposed to another language. The concept of people not being able to understand each other may be difficult for them to grasp. Consider bringing in someone who can speak in a different language. This could be a parent, member of the church, or even high school students who are taking language courses in school.

The People Build a Tall Tower

Genesis 11:1-9

Bible Point: Listen to God.

Pride. We all struggle with it, and so did the people building the tower of Babel. They were building to make a name for themselves and to avoid scattering over the face of the earth, as God wanted. Today you'll help your children understand that what God wants is more important than what we want.

Have children sit in a large circle with blocks scattered in the center. Allow them to quietly build towers with the blocks as they listen to the Bible story. Ask your children to listen for the words "Uh-oh!" When they hear "Uh-oh!" they should respond by saying, "Listen to God." Kids may want to practice it a few times before beginning the story. Your children will enjoy it even more if you are overly dramatic when you say, "Uh-oh!"

Say: **Long, long ago, in a land far from here, everyone spoke the same language. They lived in a big city. They didn't want to move to new places, even though that's what God wanted them to do. They disobeyed God.** *Uh-oh!* Lead kids in saying, "Listen to God."

These people decided to build a big, big tower so everyone would talk about their city. But that meant people didn't talk about God. *Uh-oh!* Lead kids in saying, "Listen to God."

The people made bricks and started building the tower. It got taller and taller, and people quit talking about God. *Uh-oh!* Lead kids in saying, "Listen to God."

God saw that the people were not moving to new places as he had asked. *Uh-oh!* Lead kids in saying, "Listen to God."

So God made people start talking in different languages. If they couldn't understand each other, they'd quit building the tower. They'd spread out across the world.

So God made people speak different languages. Lead small groups of children in saying the words "Jesus loves me" in the different languages that are listed in the song.

Now the people did what God wanted. *Oh, yes. This was what God wanted.* Lead the children in saying, "They listened to God."

Ask: • **What did God want the people to do?**

• **Why do you think they didn't listen to God?**

• **When have you not listened to your parents? What happened?**

Say: **When we listen to and obey our parents, we are listening to and obeying God, too.**

God Blesses Abram

cd1 track 9

The Abram Rap

Your children will enjoy acting out this chant as they repeat the words. Have your children stand up, and then begin the CD.

We're goin' on a trip, on a big, long trip. (*Repeat line while walking in place.*)

First we've gotta pack, gotta pack, pack, pack. (*Repeat line while pretending to stuff items into a suitcase.*)

Then we've gotta pray, gotta pray, pray, pray. (*Repeat line and make praying hands.*)

So what did God say, God say, God say? (*Repeat line and hold hands up.*)

We can trust him, trust him, trust him. (*Repeat line and point up.*)

Abram left with his nephew and his wife. (*Repeat line and wave goodbye.*)

First they saw the desert, saw the desert, saw the desert. (*Repeat line while shielding eyes with hand.*)

Then they heard the people, heard the people, heard the people. (*Repeat line and cup hand to ear.*)

So what did God say, God say, God say? (*Repeat line and hold hands up.*)

We can trust him, trust him, trust him. (*Repeat line and point up.*)

God told Abram to go to Canaan land. (*Repeat line and point away.*)

"I will keep you safe, keep you safe, keep you safe. (*Repeat line and hug yourself.*)

And give you lots of kids, lots of kids, lots of kids." (*Repeat line and pat air as if touching children's heads.*)

So what did God say, God say, God say? (*Repeat line and hold hands up.*)

We can trust him, trust him, trust him. (*Repeat line and point up.*)

God kept his promises and never told a lie. (*Repeat line and wag finger back and forth.*)

First he gave them food and water for their trip. (*Repeat line while pretending to eat.*)

Then he kept them safe, kept them safe, kept them safe. (*Repeat line and hug yourself.*)

Then he gave them land, gave them lots and lots of land. (*Repeat line and spread hands out, palms up.*)

So what did God say, God say, God say? (*Repeat line and hold hands up.*)

We can trust him, trust him, trust him. (*Repeat line and point up.*)

Abram Follows God

This finger play will help your children remember how Abram followed God.

Abram listened to what God said. (*Place hand behind ear and lean.*)

Abram followed to the place God led. (*Walk fingers in front of you, one hand behind the other.*)

One, two, three steps he took. (*Hold fingers up as you count.*)

Keep walking and walking until God says, "Look!" (*Shield eyes with hand and look.*)

God Blesses Abram

Genesis 12:1-8

Bible Point: We can follow God.

Abram left everything he had to obey God and follow after the promise God gave him. What faith and courage! Although young children will easily believe in God, they don't yet have the knowledge or understanding of what it means to follow God and obey him. As you share this incredible story with your children, you will be helping them understand that "obeying" is a way of "following the right choice."

Ask: • **How many of you have moved to a new place to live?**

Say: **Maybe moving was scary. But you followed and obeyed your parents, just as Abram followed and obeyed God.**

Long ago, there lived a man named Abram. He lived in a town with his father; his nephew, Lot; and his wife, Sarai. He was happy living there, and he was *very* **rich.**

But one day, God spoke to Abram and said, "Leave here and go to a new land that I will show you." But that isn't all God said. He had a very special plan for Abram. God told Abram, "I will bless you. Everyone will know your name. People everywhere will be blessed because of you." Wow! What a wonderful plan God had for Abram!

So Abram obeyed God and chose to follow him. Choose a child to be Abram and stand in front of the class. **His wife, Sarai, followed Abram.** Have Abram choose someone to be Sarai and begin forming a line behind him. **His nephew, Lot, wanted to follow Abram too.** Have Abram choose someone to be Lot and join the line to follow Abram. **But that wasn't everyone that followed Abram. Abram had many servants who went with him also.** Have Abram choose about half of the remaining children. **Abram also had many camels, sheep, and donkeys that went with him and his family.** Have Abram choose the remaining children to stand behind the rest of the children in the line.

Abram and Sarai said, "Goodbye" to all of their relatives and friends. Have kids wave goodbye. **They took their servants and all their animals and left for the new land God had promised.**

They walked and walked and walked. Have Abram lead everyone around the room, around chairs or under tables. **The roads they walked on were rough and dirty. There were no hotels to stay in overnight, so they had to put up tents or sleep out under the stars.** Lead kids in pretending to put up a tent. **They dug a hole in the ground to make a fire to cook their food.** Lead kids in pretending to shovel dirt and then eat.

Soon Abram and his family came to a wonderful land, and God said, "This is your land, Abram, your children's land, and your grandchildren's land." Abram was so happy that he stopped and prayed right there.

Have the children stop walking. Spread out a big blanket or sheet, and have the children sit down together.

Ask: • **Where are some places that your parents have taken you?**

• **What happened after you followed them to those places?**

Say: **Sarai, Lot, Abram's servants, and all Abram's animals followed Abram to their new home, and Abram followed God. Abram and his family liked their new home, and God blessed them for following him and obeying him. God had a new beautiful home waiting for Abram and his family, but they had to obey and follow God before they could see it.**

Tip From the Trenches

When speaking for Abram during the Bible story, your children will be more engaged if you use a different voice.

Isaac Is Coming

Sarah Had a Baby Boy

cd1 track 10

Sing "Sarah Had a Baby Boy" to the tune of "Mary Had a Little Lamb."

Sarah had a (*hold hands on stomach*)
Baby boy, baby boy, baby boy. (*Cradle and rock arms.*)

Sarah had a (*hold hands on stomach*)
Baby boy. (*Cradle and rock arms.*)
He brought his family joy. (*Point to happy face.*)

The Special Baby

Preschoolers love babies. Your children will delight in having their own line to repeat as you lead them in this finger play.

LEADER: **Abraham and Sarah were very, very old.**
CHILDREN: **A baby! A baby! God said they'd have a baby.** (*Pretend to rock a baby in arms.*)

LEADER: **But Sarah laughed at the thought, "A baby to hold?"**
CHILDREN: **A baby! A baby! God said they'd have a baby.** (*Pretend to rock a baby in arms.*)

LEADER: **But what God said was really true.**
CHILDREN: **A baby! A baby! God said they'd have a baby.** (*Pretend to rock a baby in arms.*)

LEADER: **They named the baby "Isaac" because he made them laugh and laugh and laugh!**
CHILDREN: **A baby! A baby! God said they'd have a baby.** (*Pretend to rock a baby in arms.*)

Isaac Is Coming

Genesis 18:1-16; 21:1-7

Bible Point: God keeps his promises.

The coming of a new baby is always a wonderful event, but when you've waited over eighty years for it to arrive, it is a spectacular *miracle*! Children enjoy surprises and are fascinated by babies smaller than themselves. Your children will enjoy singing "Rock-A-Bye, Baby" and rocking their babies as they hear how God gave Abraham and Sarah the desire of their hearts—a baby of their very own! As you teach this Bible story, you will be cultivating a sense of anticipation in your children for what God will do in their lives.

Say: **Abraham was very old—much older than any of your grandpas. His wife, Sarah, was very old too. For years and years they had wanted a baby more than anything, but now they were way too old. No one had babies when they were as old as Abraham and Sarah. God knew they wanted to have a baby, and he wanted to bless them with a baby.** Cradle arms and sing "Rock-A-Bye, Baby."

One day some visitors from far away came to talk to Abraham. Abraham and Sarah lived far away from people and didn't get very many visitors, so it was a very special celebration whenever they had visitors. Abraham noticed that the three visitors looked very important, so he bowed to them (have children stand up, bow, and then sit down) **and asked Sarah to make a big feast especially for them.** Have children stand, pretend to stir, and then sit down. **Sarah stayed inside their tent-house to prepare the**

meal. One of the visitors from God said **Abraham and Sarah would have a baby of their very own!** Cradle arms and sing "Rock-A-Bye, Baby."

Oh, but in the tent, Sarah was listening. Have kids put a hand behind one ear and listen quietly. **She couldn't believe what she heard! She laughed and thought, "I could never have a baby now. I'm way too old!"** Cradle arms and sing "Rock-A-Bye, Baby." **She laughed. She thought it was very funny to think that an old woman would have a baby.** Let each of the children take turns making their funniest laugh.

One of the visitors heard Sarah laugh and wanted to know why. After all, God could do that. Didn't she *believe* **him? Sarah realized that she had been caught listening and was afraid. Instead of telling the truth, she lied and told them that she hadn't laughed. But God knew. The visitor told her that nothing is too hard for God to do. Just wait and see!** Cradle arms

and sing "Rock-A-Bye, Baby."

A whole year went by, and guess what! Sarah did have a baby—a baby boy. Abraham and Sarah named this wonderful surprise of a baby "Isaac," which means "laughter." Baby Isaac brought laughter to all who saw him and to his mom and dad. Have children laugh all at once. **God gave Abraham and Sarah the baby for whom they had waited for so long. Nothing is impossible for God!** Cradle arms and sing "Rock-A-Bye, Baby."

Ask: • **Have you ever had to wait a very long time for a surprise? What happened?**

• **How did you feel when you had to wait?**

• **What did you do when you finally got your surprise?**

Say: **Abraham and Sarah had to wait a very long time before Isaac was born, but God kept his promise and gave them a baby of their own. God will keep his promises to you, too.**

This would be a wonderful lesson to have someone from your church bring in a baby. You could also take your children for a quick visit to your church nursery to see the babies there.

A Wife Found for Isaac

Ten Camels

cd1 track 11

Ask ten children to come stand in front of the class, or place ten stuffed animals in a row so the children can see them. Show the children how to alternate bobbing up and down as they sing "Ten Camels" to the tune of "Ninety-Nine Bottles of Pop." As you sing, begin with the number ten, then count down to zero. At the end of each verse, remove one child or stuffed animal from the line as you count down to zero camels. If you have a small class, have the children begin by holding up ten fingers and counting down.

[Ten] **camels to drink at the well,** [ten] **camels to drink.**

You draw some water and give one a sip. [Nine] **camels to drink at the well.**

Isaac Marries Rebekah

Abraham sent his servant to get Isaac a wife. *(Run fingers up arm.)*

He bounced up and down, up and down. *(Point index fingers up. With both hands in front of you, alternate bouncing hands up and down as if riding a camel.)*

"Dear God, I don't know which woman is right." *(Make praying hands.)*

He rode forward and back, forward and back. *(Point index fingers up. With both hands in front of you, alternate tipping fingers forward and back as if riding a camel.)*

Rebekah watered the camels and trusted God above. *(Point up.)*

As the camels drank, slurp and gulp, slurp and gulp. *(Cup both hands in front of you and bring hands to mouth as if drinking.)*

Rebekah rode to Isaac and fell in love. *(Hug yourself.)*

They rode forward and back, forward and back. *(Point index fingers up. With both hands in front of you, alternate tipping fingers forward and back as if riding a camel.)*

A Wife Found for Isaac

Genesis 24

Bible Point: We can trust God.

This is a story of prayer and trust. Isaac trusted his father to find a good bride for him. The servant prayed and trusted God to help him find the right woman. Rebekah heard the servant's story and trusted that God intended for her to move far away and marry Isaac, a man she had never seen. Children trust adults to provide for them every day. Each day you are helping your children to trust God, too.

Read the story enthusiastically, and lead the children in doing the motions throughout the Bible story.

Say: **Today's story is about a man named Isaac. Isaac was lonely, and his dad, Abraham, knew it was time for Isaac to get married. So Abraham sent one of his servants to bring back a good wife for Isaac.**

The servant got on his camel and began to ride. Let's pretend to ride. Pretend to ride, bouncing up and down with hands in front of you.

The servant didn't know which woman he should bring back to marry Isaac, so he bowed his head and prayed (bow head and fold hands): **"Dear God, when it is time to give water to my camels, please send the woman who should marry Isaac to help me. Amen."** Lift your head.

The servant rode all day, and his camels got thirsty. When he came to the well, young women were there to water their sheep. Say, "Baa, baa."

A beautiful woman named Rebekah walked over to the servant. She said, "I will water your camels, sir." Pretend to pour water.

The servant knew that God had answered his prayer to find a wife for Isaac. He gave Rebekah a ring for a present and asked her to ride home with him to marry Isaac.

Rebekah had never seen Isaac because he lived far away. She believed that God had chosen her to be Isaac's wife. Rebekah decided to trust God. Bow head and fold hands in prayer. **The next day, the servant and Rebekah got on the camels to ride home.** Pretend to ride, bouncing up and down with hands in front of you.

When they arrived at Isaac's home, Isaac loved Rebekah, and Rebekah loved Isaac. They were very happy. Hug yourself.

It was time to thank God for finding the right wife for Isaac. Bow head and fold hands.

Ask: • **How did Rebekah and the servant show they trusted God?**

• **How can you trust God?**

Say: **Each time they prayed, Rebekah and the servant trusted God. We can trust God each day. Let's remember to pray and thank God for always watching over us and giving us what we need.**

Jacob Tricks Esau

Tell the Truth

cd1 track 12

Sing "Tell the Truth" to the tune of "If You're Happy and You Know It." Each time you sing the verse, have the children repeat different sounds—such as clapping twice, stomping twice, or clacking their tongues twice—at the end of each line.

Oh, God is happy when we tell the truth. *(Clap hands twice.)*
Oh, God is happy when we tell the truth.

God is happy when we're truthful; when we lie it makes him sad.
Oh, God is happy when we tell the truth.

Jacob Deceives Isaac and Esau

Read the lines aloud to your children, then lead them in the motions.

Jacob got the blessing *(place hands on head as if forming a crown),*

But he used a trick. *(Shake finger "no.")*

He made a stew *(pretend to stir),*
And he made it quick. *(Stir faster.)*

He put fur on his arms *(rub hands on arms)*

And on his neck.
But blessings come from God *(place hands on head as if forming a crown, then point up),*

And not from tricks. *(Shake finger "no.")*

Jacob Tricks Esau

Genesis 25:29-34; 27:1-40

Bible Point: God wants us to tell the truth.

Your children know how it feels to want something another child also wants. As your children experience this Bible story, you'll teach them that it's better to be patient than to take what they want by trickery or force.

Before you begin, obtain one large pan, one large spoon, and three hand or bath towels. Gather one vegetable for each child: real, plastic, or a canned good. The food should be too large for accidental swallowing. Have three long strips of masking tape ready. If you have a Bible-times robe, put it on. Have the children sit in a circle so they can see, then give a vegetable to each of them. Tell the children that you will pretend to be a young man named Jacob.

Say: **My name is Jacob. You know, God wants us to always tell the truth. Let me tell you about a time I _didn't_ tell the truth—it wasn't a happy ending. You see, Isaac, my dad, told my brother, Esau, to go hunting for some meat to make a special stew to celebrate. Dad announced that it was time to give Esau his special family blessing. That meant because Esau was the oldest son, he would get most of Dad's money and land and be in charge of the family.**

Well, Mom and I didn't like that. Mom wanted the blessing for me. So she came up with a plan to trick my dad into giving _me_ the blessing instead. I went along with the plan and chose to tell a lie and trick my dad.

Let me show you what happened. I see you brought lots of great vegetables with you. You can help me make the stew. First, I set the pan on the fire. Place the pan on the floor. **When I point to you, bring your food and put it in the pot. Don't forget to stir the vegetables in the pot, and be careful of my fire!** Have the children come one at a time to put their vegetables in the pot and stir.

Smells yummy! Now I have to make Dad think that I'm my brother, Esau. Dad can't see very well, so he won't see my face. But if Dad touches my arms and neck, he'll know I'm Jacob. Hmm. What can I do to feel and smell like Esau? Let's put fur on my arms and neck so that my arms will feel like Esau's. Have the children wrap towels around your arms and neck. Secure the loose ends with tape.

I'm ready! Oh, good! My brother isn't back from hunting yet, so I will take this stew in to my dad. Pick up the pan of "stew," and carry it to a far corner of the room. Hold out a spoon of stew and pretend to talk. Return to the children, looking sad.

I did a great job of tricking Dad. He really thought I was Esau! Dad gave me the family blessing that included most of his money and land. When Esau came back and found out what I had done, he was very angry! I made Dad sad when I lied to him. I made Esau so mad that he wanted to hurt me. I had to run away for a very long time before I finally became sorry for my lie. I got what I wanted, but it didn't make me happy. And no one else was happy either. Children, always remember that God wants us to tell the truth.

Ask: • **Have you ever tricked someone and gotten in trouble for it? What happened?**

Say: **Sometimes we want to trick our friends or family because we want something really badly, but God wants us to choose to tell the truth.**

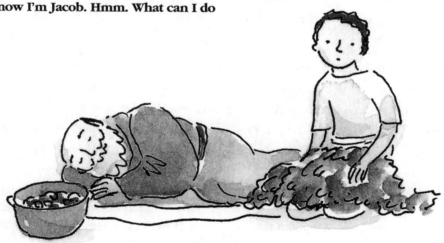

Joseph Tells His Dreams

Joseph Went to Sleep

cd1 track 13

Sing "Joseph Went to Sleep" to the tune of "A Sailor Went to Sea Sea Sea."

Joseph went to sleep, sleep, sleep. *(Place hands along side of face as if using them as a pillow.)*

He had a dream so deep, deep, deep. *(Squat down a little each time you say "deep.")*

And when he woke, he shared his dream. *(Stretch arms and pretend to yawn.)*

It made his brothers scream, scream, scream. *(Pretend to be angry and get a little louder each time you say "scream.")*

Joseph's Dreams

Go to sleep, Joseph! *(Rest head on hands.)*

Dream of wheat bowing down. *(Bend arm forward and down.)*

Go to sleep, Joseph! *(Rest head on hands.)*

Dream of stars at sundown. *(Wiggle fingers.)*

Now wake up, Joseph! *(Open hands on both sides of face.)*

Get up. Go to town! *(Stand up and walk in place.)*

Joseph Tells His Dreams

Genesis 37:1-11

Bible Point: God has an important job for everyone.

Young children are just beginning to sort facts from fiction. They may tell you about something they experienced in real life or in a dream. Acting out this Bible story will introduce your children to the fact that sometimes God used dreams to show people an important job they were about to do for God. You are building your children's confidence in God as you teach them that God has an important job for them to do.

Say: **Dreams, dreams, many dreams! Every night I dream a dream.**

I'm Jacob. I have eleven brothers. We make twelve sons for my father, Isaac. Have the children count to twelve, using their fingers.

I know my dad loves me very much. One day he gave me a colorful coat, and he often sent me to give food to my brothers. Have kids pretend to give food to each other. **He made me feel important!**

Ask: • **When have you felt important?**

Say: **When I go to sleep at night, I dream of things that seem so real. Tell me what you dream and feel.**

Ask: • **What do you dream about?**

• **How do you feel when you wake up from your dreams?**

Say: **Here's one dream I had at night as I lay on my pillow and sighed.** Lead the children in a big, long sigh.

I saw wheat. Big bundles and bunches of wheat. It wasn't growing anymore, but it was standing and bowing in the wind. Have the children stand up, sway, and bow. Then have them sit down.

I was important in that dream. I was no longer

the little bitty brother. My brothers all bowed to me, it seemed. But my dream made my brothers mad! "No way!" they said. "Just go away and be sad."

Ask: • How do you think Joseph felt when his brothers didn't like his dream?

Say: Then I had another dream. The stars all bowed. Now that is true! The sun and moon, they bowed down too. Have the children stand on tiptoes, wiggle their fingers way up high, then bend over.

I told the dreams to my brothers and Dad. But telling them just made them mad. Have kids show a mad face. God talked to me through those dreams and told me to get ready for big things. I was important to Dad and important to God. Dreams or no dreams, you, too, are important to God.

Ask: • What important things might you do for God some day?

Say: God has an important job for everyone.

Joseph Is Sold Into Slavery

Joseph's Story

Have the children walk or skip in a circle while singing "Joseph's Story" to the tune of "Camptown Races."

Joseph's brothers did something wrong. Oh, no! Oh, no! (*Stop walking. Open both hands on sides of face and look surprised.*)
Joseph's brothers did something wrong,
But we want to do what's right.
They put him in a well (*walk into the center of the circle with hands pointing down*),
Decided not to tell. (*Wag finger back and forth.*)
Joseph's brothers did something wrong (*walk back out to the larger circle*),
But we want to do what's right.

Joseph's brothers did something wrong. Oh, no! Oh, no! (*Stop walking. Open both hands on sides of face and look surprised.*)
Joseph's brothers did something wrong,
But we want to do what's right.
They made Joseph go away (*cross hands in front as if handcuffed*)
To be an Egyptian slave.
Joseph's brothers did something wrong (*walk back out to the larger circle*),
But we want to do what's right.

Joseph's Jealous Brothers

Read the verses, then lead children in the actions.

Joseph's ten brothers were jealous.
And jealousy is not very nice. (*Wag finger back and forth.*)

Just stop and think twice (*hold hand up in front of you*)

When you're not feeling right (*wag finger back and forth*),

And God will help you all day and all night. (*Make praying hands.*)

Joseph Is Sold Into Slavery

Genesis 37:12-36

Bible Point: God wants us to care about others.

Envy and jealousy appear very early in the Bible. Eve envies God's knowledge. Cain becomes jealous of Abel. Joseph's brothers are jealous of their father's attention to Joseph and the dreams God gives him. Preschool children are already familiar with feelings of jealousy. Today's story will help them understand that jealousy causes people to do wrong things, and God wants us to care about others.

Ask: • **Did you ever feel mad because someone was getting more attention than you? or someone had a toy you didn't have?**

Say: **When we feel mad because someone is getting what we don't have, we are being jealous. The Bible tells us that Joseph's dad gave him a beautiful coat. That made his brothers feel jealous and mad. Let's pretend to put on Joseph's beautiful coat.** Pretend to put on a beautiful coat.

One day Joseph went to see his brothers, who

were protecting the sheep. They grabbed Joseph and took off his coat. **Take the pretend coat off the friend sitting next to you, and throw it on the floor.** Pretend to rip off the coat and throw it on the floor.

Then they put Joseph into a hole. **Let's pretend we have a rope and we are letting Joseph down into the hole.** Pretend to lower someone down, groaning as though the person is too heavy.

The brothers began talking about what they should do with Joseph. "Let's get him!" said one brother. "No!" said another. "Let's sell him to be a slave. Then we can keep the money, and he'll be taken far away from us."

"Yes!" they said. "Get him out of that hole. **Let's sell him!**" **Let's get our ropes again and pull Joseph out of the hole.** Pretend to pull a very heavy rope out of the well.

The brothers sold Joseph to be a slave. Being a slave means that someone owns you and you can't leave. They probably tied Joseph so that he could not run away. **Let's pretend to be Joseph all tied up.** Pretend to tie a rope around a friend's crossed wrists.

Back at home, Joseph's brothers put some blood on Joseph's coat. The brothers then told their dad a lie. Have kids pretend to hold up a coat. **"Look, Dad, we found Joseph's coat. Wild animals must have hurt him."** Their dad cried for a long, long time. Pretend to cry.

Joseph's jealous brothers did some wrong things, didn't they? They sold Joseph and lied to their dad. God wants us to care for others.

Ask: • **How would you have cared for Joseph?**
• **How do you care for your family?**
Say: **God wants us to care about others.**

Joseph Forgives His Brothers

I Can Forgive Too

Sing "I Can Forgive Too" to the tune of "Ten Little Indians."

Joseph forgave all his brothers. (*Clap hands together.*)
Joseph forgave all his brothers.
Gave them grain to feed their families. (*Pretend to give things away.*)
I can forgive too. (*Pat a friend's back.*)

Joseph forgave all his brothers. (*Clap hands together.*)
Joseph forgave all his brothers.
Helped them move near him in Egypt. (*Pull pretend load.*)
I can forgive too. (*Pat a friend's back.*)

Forgiveness

Say the following finger play, and lead the children in the actions.

When someone's acting mean and makes you very sad (*point to sad mouth*),

Turn, turn, turn and forgive (*roll arms*),

And God's blessing you will give. (*Hold hands out.*)

Joseph Forgives His Brothers

Genesis 42–45

Bible Point: God wants us to forgive.

Joseph meets his brothers after having been mocked by them for his dreams, sold by them to be a slave, wrongly accused and jailed, forgotten in prison, and then raised up to be the second to Pharaoh. Joseph now realizes that God has worked a marvelous plan to save his family from starvation, and he forgives his brothers. Preschoolers aren't capable of thinking ahead and trusting that bad things can turn into good in the end. However, they can begin to ask God to forgive the people who hurt them now. As you begin encouraging your children to say, "I forgive you," when hurt by others, you are helping them begin a lifelong pattern of unconditional love for others.

Before you begin, give each child two paper plates, a red crayon, and a blue crayon. Tell kids to draw a bright happy face with the red crayon on both sides of one paper plate. Have them draw a sad face with the blue crayon on both sides of the other plate. When the children lift the plates up to you during the story, they will be able to see which face they're showing.

As you read the story, pay particular attention to your voice inflection and facial expressions. For example, you might talk slowly and softly when the story calls for being sad, or more quickly and loudly when the story is happy. Be overly dramatic, and everyone will have fun. Have children bring their plates and sit in a circle on the floor.

Say: **At different times during our Bible story, I'm going to ask you how you might feel if something happened to you. Then you can hold up the face that shows how you would feel if you were that person. God wants us to forgive. Let's see if Joseph forgives.**

Joseph had ten brothers who laughed at his dreams.

Ask: • **How would you feel if people laughed at you?** Have kids hold up the plate they choose.

• **Would you forgive?**

Say: **They were jealous of the beautiful coat Joseph got from their dad.**

Ask: • **How would you feel?** Have kids hold up the plate they choose.

• **Would you forgive?**

Say: **Joseph's brothers even sold him to be a slave. Joseph had to live far, far away and couldn't see his family.**

Ask: • **How would you feel?** Have kids hold up the plate they choose.

• **Would you forgive?**

Say: **One night, King Pharaoh had a scary dream. He asked all his wise men to tell him what it meant, but no one knew. Finally, the king heard that Joseph could help him understand his dreams. So he sent for Joseph. God showed Joseph what Pharaoh's dream meant. Pharaoh believed him and put Joseph in charge of all the food in Egypt.**

Ask: • **How would you feel if you were Joseph?** Have kids hold up the plate they choose.

Say: **Joseph's family lived a long way from Egypt, but when there was no rain to grow food, they had to travel all the way to Egypt to get more food.**

Ask: • **How would you feel if you had no food?** Have kids hold up the plate they choose.

Say: **Joseph's brothers had forgotten all about Joseph and didn't know who he was when they met him. But when Joseph saw his brothers, he recognized them right away. He remembered that they had sold him to be a slave.**

Ask: • **How would you feel if you were Joseph?** Have kids hold up the plate they choose.

• **Would you forgive?**

Say: **Joseph realized what a good life he had now that he was in Egypt. God had made all the bad things his brothers had done to him turn into something good. Joseph was a leader now in Egypt, and people bowed down to him, just as his dreams had said. Joseph was able to help his brothers now, or he could get back at them for all the mean things they had done to him.**

Ask: • **How would you feel?** Have kids hold up the plate they choose.

• **Would you forgive?**

Say: **Joseph chose to go to his brothers and say, "I'm Joseph. You should not have sold me to be a slave. But God has made me a leader so that I can help you get food. *I forgive you* for all the mean things you did to me. Go home and get my father, and we can all be together again right here in Egypt."**

Ask: • **How would you feel if you were the brothers?** Have kids hold up the plate they choose.

• **How has someone hurt you?**

• **Will you forgive that person?**

Say: **God wants us to forgive.**

God Keeps Baby Moses Safe

Baby Moses

Sing "Baby Moses" to the tune of "Ten Little Indians."

Mother put the baby in the basket. (*Pretend to place babies in baskets.*)
Mother put the baby in the basket.
Mother put the baby in the basket
And set the boat afloat.

Baby Moses floated down the Nile. (*Cup hands and move them left to right.*)
Baby Moses floated down the Nile.

Baby Moses floated down the Nile
In his basket boat.

The princess pulled the basket from the river. (*Pretend to scoop up a basket.*)
The princess pulled the basket from the river.
The princess pulled the basket from the river,
And the baby was safe at last! (*Pretend to cuddle and rock a baby.*)

God Watches Over Baby Moses

One little baby boy (*hold up one finger*)

Who brought his mommy so much joy (*laugh and snicker*)

Was placed inside a basket bed (*tuck one hand inside the other*)

And floated down a riverbed. (*Make wave motions.*)

Sister watched him float about (*shield eyes and look about*)

Until the princess shouted out (*cup hands around mouth*),

"A crying baby? It cannot be! (*Wag index finger back and forth.*)

Let's rescue him and keep him free." (*Pretend to cuddle a baby in your arms.*)

God Keeps Baby Moses Safe

Exodus 1:1–2:10

Bible Point: God takes care of us.

God kept baby Moses safe in what we would consider almost impossible circumstances. God was concerned about baby Moses, just as he is concerned with our needs. This lesson will help your children realize that God does take care of us. By allowing the children to interact with the story, you will make the story come alive to them!

38 • *Playful Songs & Bible Stories* for Preschoolers

Before you begin, instruct the children to cradle their arms as if rocking a baby every time they hear the word *baby* during the Bible story. Do the cradling motions with the children to help them remember.

Say: **Once there was a *baby*** (pretend to rock a baby) **boy who was very small. His mommy had to keep him safe from mean King Pharaoh, who wanted to hurt him. So Moses' mommy made a special basket that wouldn't sink in the water, wrapped him in a blanket, and set him safely in the basket.**

Ask: • **How would you keep your baby safe?**

Say: **Parents like to pray and ask God to keep children safe, because God takes care of you, even when you're not with your mom or dad.**

Well, the mommy then placed her *baby* (pretend to rock a baby) **in the water to float safely down the river. But the *baby*** (pretend to rock a baby) **wasn't alone. God was watching over him, and so was his big sister, Miriam. She followed the floating basket a long way down the river. She wanted to make sure her little brother was safe from the mean Pharaoh.**

Ask: • **Do you ever follow someone when they don't know you're watching?**

Say: **Miriam saw the basket floating near an area where many ladies were in the water. She wondered** if they would see the basket. But the basket kept floating down the river. Suddenly, Miriam heard a woman say she saw a basket floating. It was the princess, the mean Pharaoh's daughter. A few of the woman's servants went to get the basket.**

Ask: • **What do you think the princess will do when she finds out what's inside the basket?**

Say: **As the basket got closer, the princess could hear a small sound coming from inside. When she opened the basket, there inside was a *baby*!** Pretend to rock a baby. **She wasn't mean like the Pharaoh. She felt sorry for him. He was crying, and she wanted to make the *baby*** (pretend to rock a baby) **feel better. She couldn't take care of a hungry *baby*** (pretend to rock a baby), **so she looked around.**

Ask: • **Who do you think came out of the big, tall bushes?**

Say: **It was Miriam! Miriam knew her mother could feed her little brother. The princess agreed to let Miriam's mother take care of the *baby*** (pretend to rock a baby) **until he got older.**

The princess named the *baby* (pretend to rock a baby) **"Moses" because she found him in the water. Little Moses grew up and then went to live with the princess in a big palace. God took care of *baby*** (pretend to rock a baby) **Moses, and God will take care of us.**

Tip From the Trenches

Bring a basket with a baby doll in it to show the children. Set a long, blue sheet of bulletin board paper on the floor, and have the children sit on both sides of the "Nile River." After the Bible story, let the children take turns playing with the baby and pretending to be the Pharaoh's daughter rescuing Moses from the river.

Moses and the Burning Bush

Moses' Saga

Sing "Moses' Saga" to the tune of "Oh, Dear! What Can the Matter Be?"

(Spoken) **Moses said,**

"Oh, dear! What can the matter be? *(Hold one hand out, palm up, then the other.)*

Fire, fire, there in that burning tree! *(Bring both palms to cheeks, then point away.)*

What, what? God wants to talk to me? *(Point to yourself.)*

How could that possibly be?" *(Shrug shoulders and stand with arms out, palms up.)*

(Spoken) **God said,**

"Stop there! Take off your dirty shoes. *(Point down.)*

Moses, I want to talk to you!

Listen, I'm planning to use you *(place one hand behind ear and lean)*

To bring all my people back home." *(Motion with whole arm to come.)*

The Burning Bush

Using the finger and hand motions given below, help the children tell the story of the burning bush.

Moses was in a field one day,
Watching his sheep eat and play. *(Place hand on forehead, shielding eyes.)*

A burning bush he saw that day. *(Wiggle fingers on both sides of face.)*

God looked and said, "Let's head away. *(Motion to come.)*

Return to Egypt right away,
And help my people go, I say." *(Point away.)*

Moses and the Burning Bush

Exodus 2:11–3:20

Bible Point: God can use you.

Even though Moses begins this story by disobeying God, God still chooses to meet with Moses and to use him in setting the Israelites free. As you tell this story, you will be helping your children understand that God can use them right now.

Invite the children to stand up in a circle. Have a piece of construction paper ready for each of the children to use during the story.

Moses did something bad in Egypt, then ran away and hid. Let kids quickly pretend to hide in the room. **He walked and walked 'til he was sure he saw no pyramids.** Have kids walk in a circle a few times.

He made some friends. He took a wife. He was happy every day. Have the children find a partner and walk arm in arm in the circle.

As Moses watched his sheep one day (have kids crawl around and say, "Baa!"), **he saw a burning bush.** Place a trash can upside down in the center of the circle. Give kids red, orange, and yellow tissue paper to tape onto the bottom of the trash can to create a "burning bush." **He took off his shoes and listened to God, and God gave him a push.** Let kids take off their shoes and then sit quietly with their fingers in front of their mouths and be silent for about five to ten seconds. **God sent Moses back to Egypt.**

God wanted Moses to obey.

God loved the Israelites, it's true. But Moses said, "No way!" Have kids point to their hearts. **I can't talk to Pharaoh! I'll make mistakes. I don't know what to say!"** Have kids place their hands over their mouths.

"That's all right," God said, "Your brother will talk in your place." Have kids shake hands with a friend next to them. **"Now go, and I will use *you* to set my people free!"** Let kids walk in a small circle, holding hands. **So Moses left and walked and walked, and one day, finally, it happened just as God had said—God set his people free!**

Have kids throw their hands up as they step back from the circle.

Ask: • **How did God use Moses?**
• **How can God use you?**

Moses Pleads With Pharaoh

God Told Moses

Have your children stand up and do the motions for the verses. Sing "God Told Moses" to the tune of "Did You Ever See a Lassie?"

God told Moses, "Take my people (rock back
    and forth holding hands with a partner)
From Pharaoh—he's evil!"
God told Moses, "Take my people
From Pharaoh right now!"

So Moses told Pharaoh *(one partner points away),*
"The Israelites must go."
But old Pharaoh, he said,
"Oh, no! They're staying with me." *(Second part-*
    ner points down.)

God sent frogs and gnats and locusts *(act like*
    frogs and flies)
And flies and diseases.
Finally Pharaoh changed his mind
When his firstborn son died.

So Pharaoh told Moses *(skip in a circle),*
"Take God's people—please go!"
So the Israelites were free
To go worship the Lord.

God Is Strong!

God always takes care of his people! Use this finger play to help your children learn that our God watches out for his people.

Pharaoh was a stubborn man. *(Place hands on*
    hips and look mad.)

"They're my slaves! I have plans!" *(Point to*
    yourself.)

But God was strong, and he did show *(show*
    strong arms)

That what he says most certainly does go.
(Show thumbs up.)

Moses Pleads With Pharaoh

Exodus 7:14–12:30

Bible Point: God is strong.

We have seen how God helped the Israelites before, and today we can see it again. Help your preschoolers understand that God was the one who set the Israelites free. By sharing this lesson with your children, you are teaching them that God is stronger than anything or anyone.

Before you begin, gather a glass of water, red food coloring, and a large paintbrush. Instruct the children to shake their heads and their fingers as if saying "no." Tell them to listen for the key phrase, "But Pharaoh didn't change his mind."

Say: **Pharaoh kept God's people, the Israelites, in Egypt for a very long time. He made them build beautiful palaces and tall, tall pyramids and wouldn't let them leave. He thought he was the strongest king ever, but there was someone stronger. He made God's people slaves and worked them harder and harder all the time. Every day the people cried to God to set them free. Then one day God said, "That's enough of mean King Pharaoh! I'll send Moses to set you free."**

Moses prayed to God for help. Have the children fold their hands and pray, "Dear God, help me set your people free." **So God turned all of Egypt's water red.** Place a drop of red food coloring in a glass of water.

Moses went to Pharaoh and asked, "Will you let my people go?" But Pharaoh didn't change his mind. Have kids place their hands on their hips and say, "No way!"

Moses prayed to God for help. Have the children fold their hands and pray, "Dear God, help me set your people free." **So God sent a bunch of frogs to cover the land. They were everywhere the Egyptians didn't want them to be!** Have kids hop around like frogs.

Moses went to Pharaoh and asked, "Will you let my people go?" But Pharaoh didn't change his mind. Have kids place their hands on their hips and say, "No way!"

Moses went to God for help. Have the children fold their hands and pray, "Dear God, help me set your people free." **So God sent little gnats and flies that no one liked.** Let kids pretend to be gnats and fly around the circle. Then sit down.

Moses went to Pharaoh and asked, "Will you let my people go?" But Pharaoh didn't change his mind. Have

kids place their hands on their hips and say, "No way!"

Moses prayed to God for help. Have the children fold their hands and pray, "Dear God, help me set your people free." **So God made the daytime into night-time for three days.** Have the children place their hands in their laps, count to three, and then sit up.

Moses went to Pharaoh and asked, "Will you let my people go?" But Pharaoh didn't change his mind. Have kids place their hands on their hips and say, "No way!"

Pharaoh was a very stubborn man, but God told Moses to get ready. God would show everyone who was stronger.

Moses prayed to God for help. Have the children fold their hands and pray, "Dear God, help me set your people free." **So God told his people, the Israelites, to put a red mark over their doors and he would keep them safe from the very last plague.** Let the children take turns using a dry paintbrush and pretending to paint the wall red.

In the morning, all the Israelites were safe, but the Egyptians were very sad. Moses went to Pharaoh and asked, "Will you let my people go?" This time Pharaoh was mad and told Moses to get his people and GO! Lead the children in a cheer: "Yeah!"

Ask: • **How would you feel if you were Moses and Pharaoh finally told you to go?**

• **How would you celebrate if you were a slave and God set you free?**

• **How can God be strong for you?**

Say: **God is stronger than anyone or anything, and he will always be with you.**

Moses Crosses the Red Sea

Our God Helps Us

Sing "Our God Helps Us" to the tune of "London Bridge."

God holds back the big Red Sea *(stand with feet apart and arms outstretched)*,
Big Red Sea, big Red Sea. *(Lean back and forth.)*
God holds back the big Red Sea *(stand with feet apart and arms outstretched)*;
Our God helps us. *(Point upward, then clap one time.)*

Hurry now and hop across *(hop in place)*,
Hop across, hop across. *(Hop in place.)*
Hurry now and hop across *(hop in place)*;
Our God helps us. *(Point upward, then clap one time.)*

Crossing the Red Sea

What a fun story to tell children! Use enthusiasm as you teach this finger play. Get your children excited about God's mighty power!

Pharaoh let the people go. *(With thumbs up, throw your hands over your shoulders.)*

The Israelites were free! *(Stretch out arms.)*

Through the desert they did go *(walk fingers up arm)*

And then camped out by the sea. *(Interlock fingers and make rolling motion with hands.)*

Pharaoh changed his mind, you know.
The people were afraid. *(Show scared face.)*

But God did make the sea to part *(place hands together over head, then separate them)*

And gave them a new start. *(Place hands on heart.)*

Moses Crosses the Red Sea

Exodus 13:17–14:31

Bible Point: God can do anything.

God continually amazes his people, and this story is yet another example. The Red Sea actually parted to spare God's people from the Egyptians. What a fun story to share with your class! As your children experience this Bible story, they will see that God can do anything.

Before you begin, gather one white pillow and a piece of red tissue paper for each of your children. Your children will enjoy repeating the story more than once.

Say: **Pharaoh let the people go, just like he said he would. Pharaoh let the people go; they left as fast as they could!** Have the children stand, walk quickly in a circle a few times, and then sit down.

They didn't need to worry, though. They had the very best guide. They didn't need to worry, though, 'cause God was by their side. Have kids link arms with the children next to them.

God sent his people a big cloud to guide them through the day. Let the children pass a white pillow around the circle. **God sent his people fire by night to help them light their way.** Give kids red tissue paper to sway above their heads and then crumple to make fire sounds.

Pharaoh began to wonder, though, "Why did I let them leave? I want the Israelites back with me. I'll get them, wait and see." Have kids stand up, place their hands on their hips, and stomp their feet.

The Israelites looked behind them, and whom do you think they saw? They saw the Egyptian army that looked so big and tall! Spread arms wide and then point up.

God parted the Red Sea, from the left to the right. Bring one arm out, then the other. **God separated the waters. God parted the Red Sea and showed us his might.** Have kids show their strong arms.

Ask: • **What amazing things did God do in the Bible story?**

• **What are some other things that God can do?**

Say: **God is with us, watching over us all the time. He was with the Israelites all during the day, and he was with them guiding them all through the night. Then he parted the waters and kept them safe from Pharaoh's army. God can do anything for you, too.**

God Gives Moses the Ten Commandments

cd1 track 20

God Loves Us

Sing this version of "God Loves Us" to the original tune of "Jesus Loves Me."

Honor God with all your might. *(Point to heaven.)*
Serving idols isn't right. *(Shake finger and head.)*
Treat God's name with thoughtfulness. *(Touch finger to temple.)*
God made the Sabbath day for rest. *(Rest head on hands.)*

God gave us ten rules. *(Hold up ten fingers.)*
God gave us ten rules. *(Hold up ten fingers.)*
God gave us ten rules *(hold up ten fingers)*
Because he loves us so! *(Hug yourself.)*

Honor mom and daddy, too *(point to right, then left)*;
Remember how much they love you. *(Hug yourself.)*
No stealing, murder, jealousy. *(Hold up one finger for each commandment.)*
Don't lie about your friend, you see. *(Put arms around two friends.)*

God gave us ten rules. *(Hold up ten fingers.)*
God gave us ten rules. *(Hold up ten fingers.)*
God gave us ten rules *(hold up ten fingers)*
Because he loves us so! *(Hug yourself.)*

Ten Special Rules

Your children will enjoy using their ten fingers as they repeat this finger play.

Ten special rules God wants us to obey. *(Hold up ten fingers.)*

One is to love only our God. *(Hold up one finger.)*

The second, "Put God first." *(Hold up two fingers.)*

The third rule says, "Respect God's name." *(Hold up three fingers.)*

The fourth is "Take a rest." *(Hold up four fingers.)*

The fifth your mom and dad will like. It says, "Obey; be blessed." *(Hold up five fingers.)*

The sixth rule says to never kill or hurt a friend. *(Hold up six fingers.)*

The seventh, "Love one husband or one wife." *(Hold up seven fingers.)*

The eighth says, "Never steal from anyone." *(Hold up eight fingers.)*

And the ninth says you shouldn't lie 'cause God will hear you by and by. *(Hold up nine fingers.)*

The last good rule, the tenth, it's true, says, "Be happy with all you have, for God will give you all you need." Be sure, it's guaranteed!

(Hold up ten fingers.)

God Gives Moses the Ten Commandments

Exodus 19:16–20:21

Bible Point: God give us rules because he loves us.

Before you begin, seat your children in three groups. Have the children in the "Thunder" group practice stomping their feet. Have the children in the "Lightning" group clap their hands loudly. Have the children in the "Trumpet" group place their hands around their mouths and pretend to blow trumpets. Remind the children that they are to be very quiet until they hear their words—*thunder, lightning,* or *trumpet.*

Say: **This was a big day! God was going to give some special rules to his people that we still use today. Moses had walked a very long way up the mountain, and down below, the people waited. They saw fire and smoke way up on top. They knew God was on that mountain.**

All of a sudden, there was *thunder*. Have the Thunder group make its noise.

Then there was *lightning*. Have the Lightning group make its noise.

Next there may have been a *trumpet* blast. Have the Trumpet group make its noise.

God wanted his people to listen! He was giving Moses ten good rules to make their lives happier.

The first good rule was to love God more than anything or anyone else. Have kids hold up one finger and then hug themselves.

The second rule was to worship only God. Have kids hold up two fingers and then point up.

The third was to speak nicely when using God's name. Have kids hold up three fingers and then touch their mouths.

The fourth was to rest on the Sabbath day. Have kids hold up four fingers and then lean on a friend's shoulder.

The fifth rule was to love your mommy and daddy. Have kids hold up five fingers and then hug themselves.

The sixth rule was to never hurt anyone. Have kids hold up six fingers and then stroke a friend's arm.

The seventh rule was to love one husband or one wife. Have kids hold up seven fingers and then show one index finger, then the other.

The eighth rule was to never steal. Have kids hold up eight fingers and then put one of their hands behind their backs.

The ninth rule was to never lie and always tell the truth. Have kids hold up nine fingers and then place their hands around their mouths and shout, "Tell the truth!"

And the tenth and last good rule was to be happy and thankful with all you have. Have kids hold up ten fingers and then take turns saying one thing they are thankful for.

Again, God sent *thunder* (have the Thunder group make its noise), ***lightning*** (have the Lightning group make its noise), **and a *trumpet* blast.** (Have the Trumpet group make its noise.)

Ask: • **What good rule do you like to obey?**

• **What rules are hard to obey?**

Say: **God loved his people. He wanted what was best for them. God gave his people ten good rules so they could love him and obey his words. God gave us these same ten rules so we could love him and obey him too.**

Balaam's Donkey Talks

Come and See

Sing "Come and See" to the tune of "The Mulberry Bush."

Come and see what God has done, God has done, God has done. (*Hold hands and walk in a circle.*)
Come and see what God has done (*continue in a circle*)—
Mighty, wonderful things. (*Stop walking and drop hands.*)

Wonderful, awesome, God is great! God is good! God is great! (*Wave hands in air.*)
Wonderful, awesome, God is great! (*Wave hands in air.*)
What a mighty God! (*Join hands and walk in a circle.*)

The Talking Donkey

Use your enthusiasm to build excitement about this talking donkey. Help the children pick one of their fingers to be the "donkey." Let them decorate their fingers with washable markers. Their donkeys will go home with them, and hopefully, so will this finger play!

One little donkey giving a ride. (*Hold up one finger and bounce it up and down.*)

When he saw an angel, he tried to hide! (*Hide finger behind opposite hand.*)

Balaam was upset. What was wrong with his pet? (*Shrug shoulders.*)

He used to be so good. Now he won't do what he should. (*Wag finger.*)

Then Balaam saw what the donkey had seen. (*Place hand over eyes.*)

"Now I understand," he said. "Now I know what you mean." (*Touch finger to side of head.*)

Then Balaam said, as he knew he should say (*point to mouth*),

"I will do what God tells me—today and every day!" (*Point up.*)

Balaam's Donkey Talks

Numbers 22

Bible Point: Do what God says.

God continually amazes his people, and this Bible story will truly amaze your children. This story proves that God is all-powerful and has dominion over all. Your children will see yet another example of God's power.

Before you begin, have each of your children make a simple paper-bag puppet out of a lunch sack, markers, two giant wiggly eyes, two long ears cut out of construction paper, and white glue. Then let the children use their donkeys to act out the following Bible story.

Say: **The Israelites traveled to the land of Moab, where King Balak ruled.** Have the children hold up their donkeys and bob them up and down in front of them.

The Israelites set up their tents and began to live there. But King Balak didn't want the Israelites to stay in his land. He wanted them to leave, so he sent one of his servants to ask a fortuneteller, Balaam to put a curse on the Israelites so they would leave. King Balak even offered Balaam a lot of money so he would do it. Balaam had a hard time deciding what to do. The king was going to give him lots and lots of money, but he would have to tell the Israelites to get out of Moab.

Ask: • **What would you do if you were Balaam? Would you take the money or stand by the Israelites?**

Say: **Balaam had a hard choice to make, so he prayed and asked God what he should do. God told Balaam, "Do what I tell you to do." So Balaam decided to get on his donkey and head for Moab.** Have the children hold up their donkeys and bob them up and down in front of them.

As Balaam was traveling to Moab. God's angel stood in the middle of the road and stopped the donkey so he couldn't go by. God had sent his angel to stop Balaam because God wanted his people, the Israelites, to live in Moab for a long time. Balaam couldn't see the angel, but Balaam's donkey could. **The donkey was afraid!** Have the children hold up their donkeys and shake them as if the donkeys are afraid.

The donkey kept moving away from the angel. Have the children back their donkeys up toward their bodies. **This made Balaam mad! He couldn't get his donkey to move forward no matter what he tried.** Have the children push the backs of their donkeys with their other hands as if trying to move them.

Ask: • **How would you feel if your donkey wouldn't obey you?**

Say: **All of a sudden, the donkey started to talk! "Why are you hurting me? I'm the same donkey you ride every day. You know I always obey you."**

Finally Balaam realized that there must be a reason his donkey wouldn't obey, and there it was. Now Balaam could see the angel standing in front of them, blocking their way. Balaam remembered that he had prayed and asked God what he should do.

Ask: • **What do you think God's answer to Balaam's prayer was?**

Say: **Balaam said, "I will do only what the Lord tells me to do." So Balaam turned around and didn't go to Moab to curse the Israelites. Balaam obeyed what God said.** Have the children turn their donkeys around and bob them up and down as if returning home.

Joshua Sends Spies Into Canaan

We Are Spying

Sing "We Are Spying" to the tune of "Did You Ever See a Lassie?"

We are spying in the Promised Land (*put hands around eyes like glasses*),
The Promised Land, the Promised Land.
We are spying in the Promised Land
To see what is there. (*Shade eyes with hand.*)

We see big trees growing (*crouch down, then stand up slowly*),
Great big trees growing. (*Slowly reach arms to sky.*)
We are spying in the Promised Land (*put hands around eyes like glasses*)
To see what is there. (*Shade eyes with hand.*)

We are spying in the Promised Land (*put hands around eyes like glasses*),
The Promised Land, the Promised Land.
We are spying in the Promised Land (*put hands around eyes like glasses*)
To see what is there. (*Shade eyes with hand.*)

We see giant grapes a-swinging (*bend over and swing arms loosely*),
Giant grapes a-swinging. (*Continue swinging arms.*)
We are spying in the Promised Land (*put hands around eyes like glasses*)
To see what is there. (*Shade eyes with hand.*)

Two Spies

This is a fun and simple finger play to help children learn that God keeps his promises.

Two spies were sent into Jericho one day.
(*Hold up two fingers.*)

They were told to listen to what the people would say. (*Place hand behind ear and lean.*)

There they found one lady who told them the news. (*Cup hands around mouth.*)

They knew they could trust her, that her words were true. (*Place finger in front of mouth.*)

The two spies returned to tell Joshua the news (*cup hands around mouth*):

"The people are afraid of us; what God said is true!" (*Point up.*)

God does keep his promises to me and to you!
(*Point to yourself and then to the children.*)

Joshua Sends Spies Into Canaan

Joshua 2

Bible Point: God keeps his promises.

Our God is a god of his word. Joshua learns that the people of Jericho fear the Israelites, just as God said they would. When you share this story with your children, they will experience another example of how God keeps his promises to his people. Have the children do the motions with you as you read the Bible story.

Say: **Moses was a very old man.** Have the children stand up, walk in a circle as if leaning on canes, and then sit down. **Moses was getting too old to lead God's people, so God sent a man named Joshua to be the new leader of God's people.** Have the children salute.

One of the first things God told Joshua to do was to take over the city of Jericho. So Joshua sent two spies into Jericho. Have the children stand up and pretend to climb up a tall wall and sneak around corners.

When the spies went to Jericho, they watched the people and listened to what they said. The spies wanted to know if the people were afraid of the Israelites or if they were going to be brave and fight them.

Ask: • **What do you think the spies heard the people say?**

Say: **They met a nice lady who let them hide in her house.** Have the children put their hands in front of their eyes and peek out. **She protected them and kept them safe. She also told them all that they needed to know. They could trust her because she wanted to believe in God too. She knew God was with them.**

Before they left, the spies told her to hang a red rope in her window and God would keep her safe. Then the spies left and went back to Joshua and told God's people that the people of Jericho were afraid of the Israelites because God was with them. "God is with us," they said. "We can take this city for God!" Joshua believed the spies and knew God would keep his promise and give the city of Jericho to them.

Ask: • **How would you have felt if you were one of the spies?**

• **What has someone promised you?**

Say: **You can believe God when he says something. God always keeps his promises.**

Jericho's Walls Come Down

Oh, When We March

Sing "Oh, When We March " to the tune of "When the Saints Go Marching In."

Oh, when we march around that wall *(march in place)*,

Oh, when we march around that wall *(march in place)*,

We know that God will give us the victory *(point to heaven)*

When we march around that wall. *(March in place.)*

Oh, when we blow our trumpets loud *(pretend to blow trumpet)*,

Oh, when we blow our trumpets loud *(pretend to blow trumpet)*,

We know that God will give us the victory *(point to heaven)*

When we blow our trumpets loud. *(Pretend to blow trumpet.)*

And the Walls Came Tumbling Down!

This is a fun finger play that your children will enjoy and that will help them remember the Bible story.

God keeps his promises each and every day *(point up)*,

Just like he did for the Israelites that very special day. *(Hug yourself.)*

He told them to march around Jericho's wall *(march fingers up arm)*

And take the great city although it seemed tall. *(Lift arms up high.)*

They obeyed God and marched around the city once every day for seven days: **one** *(hold up one finger and make circles in the air)*, **two** *(hold up two fingers and make circles in the air)*, **three** *(hold up three fingers and make circles in the air)*, **four** *(hold up four fingers and make circles in the air)*, **five** *(hold up five fingers and make circles in the air)*, **six.** *(Hold up six fingers and make circles in the air.)*

The seventh day they marched around the city seven times *(count to seven, holding up seven fingers and making circles in the air)*,

Blew their trumpets *(pretend to blow a trumpet)*,

And the walls fell down! *(Bring hands down.)*

Jericho's Walls Come Down

Joshua 6

Bible Point: Nothing is impossible for God.

Ever encounter a situation that seemed impossible? The Israelites thought the Jericho wall was an impossible situation, too. This Bible story will help your children remember that nothing is impossible for God.

Before you begin, build a wall using cardboard bricks or other small cardboard boxes. Roll up pieces of paper like cones to create trumpets for your children. Have your children sit in a circle around the wall. Help kids practice saying the CHILDREN lines with the motions, and then begin the Bible story.

CHILDREN: **God is going to do it! God is going to win!** (*Pump fist in the air.*)

Say: **God was going to give Jericho to his people, but the city of Jericho had a big wall around it. It was very, very tall and very, very wide. What were they going to do?**

Ask: • **How do you think they could get past the tall wall?**

CHILDREN: **God is going to do it! God is going to win!** (*Pump fist in the air.*)

Say: **God had a plan. He told the Israelites to march around the wall once each day, and then on the seventh day, they marched around the wall seven times.**

Have children stand up in a circle and walk around a table or a chair seven times, counting each time they pass the starting point. When you say the number seven, have them stop and stand in place.

CHILDREN: **God is going to do it! God is going to win!** (*Pump fist in the air.*)

Say: **On the seventh day, God told the Israelites to blow their trumpets as loud as they could.** Give children paper trumpets, and let them march around the table one more time, blowing their trumpets as they march.

CHILDREN: **God is going to do it! God is going to win!** (*Pump fist in the air.*)

Say: **Guess what God did! The walls fell down, just as God said they would! Nothing is impossible for God.**

CHILDREN: **God is going to do it! God is going to win!** (*Pump fist in the air.*)

God Gives Gideon Victory

God Called Gideon

cd1 track 24

Sing "God Called Gideon" to the tune of "Hush, Little Baby."

God called Gideon for his plan. *(Touch mouth.)*
But Gideon said, "I'm not the right man."
   (Shake head "no.")
God said, "Gideon, trust in me. *(Touch heart.)*
I will help you; you will see." *(Point to sky, then
   to eyes.)*

God called Gideon for his plan. *(Touch mouth.)*
Gideon knew he was the right man. *(Nod head
   "yes.")*
God said, "Gideon, trust in me." *(Touch heart.)*
Gideon trusted and believed. *(Hold both arms up
   toward sky.)*

Gideon's Army

Children enjoy finger plays, especially when they learn a Bible truth. Help your children remember that God is there to listen to us when we call on him. Enjoy this finger play with your class.

Gideon had an army with many, many men.
   (Salute.)

God said trust him again and again. *(Point up,
   then roll arms.)*

Take them to the water and see how they
   drink. *(Pretend to drink.)*

A smaller army's better, don't you think? *(Shrug
   shoulders.)*

God wanted the army smaller so they would
   trust him. *(Point up.)*

God's army was ready, now only three hundred to win. *(Salute.)*

They marched to the camp, gave a shout of
   surprise *(place hands around mouth)*,

Blew trumpets *(pretend to blow trumpet)*,

Smashed pitchers *(clap hands loudly)*,

And scared all of those guys! *(Point away.)*

God Gives Gideon Victory

Judges 6:1-16; 7:1-24

Bible Point: Trust God.

Even though the Israelites continually disappointed God, God helped them when they cried to him. He gave Gideon directions, and Gideon followed them. Good things happen when we trust God! Encourage your class to be like Gideon and trust God.

Before you begin, have the children wash their hands or use wet wipes. Have two bowls filled with small bear cookies (animal crackers work). Place at least six bear cookies per child in the bowl that will represent the Israelites, and place a noticeably larger amount in the larger bowl. Invite the children to sit in a large circle around the bowls.

Say: **The Israelites didn't listen very well, and God wasn't happy with them. For seven years, the Israelites were sad. Then they remembered God and finally asked him for help.**

Ask: • **How do you ask God for help?**

Say: **The people in the land where the Israelites lived were very mean to the Israelites, so God sent Gideon to help them.** Point to the bowl that has more bear cookies, and tell the children that this bowl of bear cookies is the mean people's army. **God called Gideon a mighty warrior, and Gideon asked many men to join his army.** Point to the second, smaller bowl, and tell the children that they will pretend that these bears are Gideon's army.

Ask: • **How many men do you think it takes to make a big, *huge* army?**

Say: **Well, Gideon thought he had big army—he had twenty-two *thousand* men! But Gideon knew the people they had to fight had an even bigger army** (point to the larger bowl), **so Gideon's army would never win. But God said Gideon had too many men. "Trust me," God said again and again. "Ask the brave men to stay, and see how many are left."**

Each time men left, the army got smaller and smaller. Have the children take turns coming up and taking two bear cookies from the smaller bowl back to their seats to eat them while they listen.

Gideon's army was much smaller now, but God said his army was still too big. This time God told Gideon to take the men down to the river to see how they drank. If they scooped up the water with their hands, they were to leave the army and go home. Have kids pretend to scoop water with their hands. **But if they drank the water with their tongues, they could stay.** Have the kids pretend to lap up water like dogs. **Lots more men left this time!** Have the children come up, take three bear cookies each from the smaller bowl, and then return to their seats to eat them.

Now Gideon only had three hundred men left! Point out the difference between the amounts of bear cookies in the bowls.

Ask: • **Do you think Gideon's army will win with a smaller army? Why or why not?**

Say: **God was happy with Gideon's tiny, little army. Now Gideon's army was ready. Gideon and all the Israelites had to trust God for the victory now! But God hadn't finished. He told Gideon that the army should carry trumpets and clay pitchers *instead* of swords. That's the craziest thing! How could anyone win a battle without fighting with weapons?**

Ask: • **Would you trust God to win a battle without any weapons? Why or why not?**

Say: **The battle plan was finally set. The Israelites were to sneak up on the army during the night with trumpets and clay pitchers in their hands. The army blew their trumpets.** Have kids pretend to blow trumpets and make trumpet sounds. **The army shouted and broke the clay pitchers.** Have kids clap their hands and yell. **And God gave Gideon's army the victory! They won the battle that day with only a small amount of men and no weapons. We can trust God to take care of our little everyday battles, too.**

God Gives Samson a Special Gift

Good Gifts

Sing "Good Gifts" to the tune of "I've Been Working on the Railroad."

God's been givin' good gifts to us *(stretch hands in front of you)*;
We've sure come a long way! *(March in place.)*
God's been givin' good gifts to us *(stretch hands in front of you)*;
We can do more every day. *(March in place.)*

Can't ya see how big we're growin'? *(Squat down and jump up.)*
We're doing much more than before. *(March in place.)*
God is helpin' us grow stronger *(make muscles)*
So we can serve him more! *(March in place.)*

Samson's Special Gift

What an interesting story—a man with strength in his hair! God can do anything! This is a fun finger play to teach your class about Samson and his special gift.

Samson was a strong man. *(Show strong arms.)*

A mighty man was he.
He promised God he would obey *(point up)*,

So the gift of strength he had each day. *(Show strong arms.)*

God Gives Samson a Special Gift

Judges 15:9-16; 16:4-30

Bible Point: God can use you.

Preschoolers love to hear the story about Samson and his mighty strength. God gives his people all kinds of gifts, and Samson's gift was his amazing strength. Enjoy sharing this story with your children. You can be assured that as they grow, they will begin to realize the many gifts and talents they have and will remember that their gifts come from God.

Say: **God gave a man named Samson a secret strength that made him stronger than anyone else in the land.**

Ask: • **Who is the strongest person you know?**
• **What do you think makes people strong?**

Say: **Samson was an Israelite who promised to serve God from the time he was very little. One thing he promised God was that he would never cut his hair. He must have had very long hair by the time he was a grown man. Let's find out if any of you have shorter or longer hair than Samson.**

Let children who want to come stand by you and line up in order of hair length. Starting with the person who has the shortest hair, say, "Do you think Samson's hair was shorter or longer?" Continue doing the same with each of the children in line. Thank the children for helping you, then let them return to their seats.

Say: **Samson was just an ordinary man, maybe like your dads, but God gave him a special gift of strength so that he could serve God in a big way.**

Everyone wanted to know what made him strong, but Samson wouldn't tell. The Israelites' enemies especially wanted to know what made Samson so strong because they wanted to stop him. They were always trying to think up ways to trick him into telling them.

One time Samson's enemies told him they would kill him if he didn't tell them the secret of his strength, but Samson wouldn't tell. They even tried to tie him up, but Samson wouldn't tell. He just broke the ropes, laughed at them, and ran away.

Samson's girlfriend, Delilah, tried to trick him into telling her the secret of his mighty strength. Many times Delilah tied up Samson, and every time Samson broke the ropes.

Help the children form trios for this fun game. Have two of the partners form a bridge with their arms, and let the third child stand in the center, pretending to be Samson. Tell the two partners to "lock" their arms around "Samson" so he can't get away. At the end of the following song, tell Samson that he or she can break out of the "locked" arms. Sing the following song to the tune of "London Bridge." (You'll only be singing the verse part.) Repeat the game three times, giving everyone a chance to be Samson.

What's the secret of your strength,
Of your strength, of your strength?
What's the secret of your strength?
Tell me now!

Say: **Delilah begged and pleaded, cried and moaned, but Samson wouldn't tell her the secret of his mighty strength. Let's beg and plead.** Have the children pretend to beg, getting down on their knees with praying hands and saying, "Pleeeeease!" **Let's all cry and moan.** Encourage them to whine and cry as they continue on their knees saying, "Pleeeease!"

She was going to find out the secret of Samson's strength *no matter what!*

Finally, one night when Delilah was begging and pleading with Samson to tell her the secret of his strength again, Samson finally gave up. "Stop! Enough! I'll tell you, already! The secret is my long hair. If I cut my hair, my strength will be gone."

Ask: • **That night, what do you think Delilah did?**

Say: **Delilah told her friends (who were also Samson's enemies) to come stand on the other side of the door and wait for her to yell. Then they could come in and get Samson. So that night, Delilah tied up Samson again and this time cut his hair while he was asleep. When she yelled, Samson's enemies came running in.**

Ask: • **Do you think Samson broke the ropes and got away this time? Why or why not?**

• **How do you think Samson felt when he couldn't get away?**

Say: **Samson had lost his strength. He couldn't get away no matter how hard he struggled. Samson was as weak as any other man that lived there in the town. Samson's enemies hurt him and tied him up. It was very sad.**

Samson was sorry that he had trusted Delilah and broken his promise to God. He asked God to forgive him and use him again to win the victory over his enemies.

Ask: • **What do you think God did?**

Say: **God forgave Samson and gave him back his mighty strength, and Samson won a victory for all of Israel that day.**

Ask: • **What are some ways God can use you? at home? at church?**

Say: **God used Samson in a mighty way, and God can you use in a mighty way too.**

Ruth Trusts God

I Hope in God

Sing "I Hope in God" to the tune of "The Ants Go Marching."

cd1 track 26

I hope in God; I trust in God. *(Raise right hand, then left.)*
Hurray, hurray! *(Jump up on each word.)*
I hope in God; I trust in God. *(Raise right hand, then left.)*
Hurray, hurray! *(Jump up on each word.)*
God will never let me go. *(Shake head and hug yourself.)*

He has great plans for me, I know. *(Tap temple with index finger.)*
And so I can hope and trust *(raise right hand, then left)*
In God. *(Point up.)*
Hurray, hurray! *(Jump up on each word.)*

Ruth and Naomi Trusted God

Your children will delight in repeating this fun finger play over and over.

Ruth and Naomi trusted God. *(Make praying hands.)*

If you think so, give a nod. *(Nod head "yes.")*

Ruth and Naomi trusted God. *(Make praying hands.)*

God took care of them, so let's applaud. *(Clap your hands.)*
Ruth and Naomi trusted God. *(Make praying hands.)*

Ruth Trusts God

Ruth 1–4

Bible Point: We can trust God.

The story of Ruth and her commitment to Naomi is one of the Bible's most touching stories. Preschoolers will learn that God rewards faithfulness. Just as Ruth committed herself to Naomi, you have committed yourself to teaching. God's blessings to you for your dedication. Because of your faithfulness, the children to whom you minister will flourish.

Before you begin, have the children wash their hands or use wet wipes. Have the children sit at a table or in a large circle on the floor, close enough to reach the center. Place a large bowl of pretzel sticks in the center of your children, along with a smaller bowl of wheat cereal squares. Tell the children they'll be helping you act out the Bible story with pretzel sticks. Hold up one pretzel stick at a time when you add people to the story and then lay the pretzel sticks down as people leave the story. At the end, let the children eat all the pretzels.

Say: **A long time ago in Bethlehem, there was a woman named Naomi.** Have each child take one pretzel stick from the bowl and hold it up. **Naomi married a nice man, and she was very happy.** Have each child take another pretzel stick and hold it up. **Naomi and her husband had one bouncing baby boy. Happy Naomi got even happier.** Have each child take another pretzel stick and hold it up. **Then they had another bubbly, bouncing baby boy.** Have each child take another pretzel stick and hold it up. **Naomi never dreamed she could be so happy. One, two, three, four in the happy family.** Have kids count their pretzel people.

The boys grew up, and they got married to two sweet ladies. Have each child take two more pretzel sticks and hold them up. **Now Naomi had a family of one, two, three, four, five, six.** Have kids count their sticks.

One day something very sad happened. The father died. Have each child put one pretzel stick down. **Later on, the two boys died.** Have each child put two pretzel sticks down. **Now there were only one, two, and three in Naomi's family.** Have kids count the sticks in their hands. **Naomi never dreamed she could be so sad.**

She lived far away from all her friends and the rest of her family, and she felt lonely. Naomi said, "I'm going home. You girls can stay here with your own families." Naomi kissed them goodbye, and they all cried. Have each child pick up one pretzel from his or her hand and touch it to the others as if giving them a kiss, and then place it back in his or her hand.

One daughter said, "OK, goodbye." Have each child put down one pretzel stick with the others.

Naomi started to walk away, all alone. She had never been lonelier. But Ruth ran to her and said, "I will stay with you. Wherever you go, I will go, and your God will be my God."

Ask: • **How do you think Naomi felt when she heard that?**

Say: **Ruth helped Naomi feel happier. There were only two left in Naomi's little family, but she felt better already!** Have kids count the sticks left in their hands.

Ruth and Naomi walked and walked for days. By the time they got to Naomi's town, they were hungry and had no more food left. So Ruth went out to a field to pick up grain that no one wanted. She knew that if she picked up enough grain, she could grind it into flour and make bread for her and Naomi to eat.** Have each child pick up a few pieces of wheat cereal. **Ruth brought the food home to Naomi. They made bread and had a good dinner.**

Boaz, the man who owned the field, saw Ruth and wanted to help her. Naomi knew Boaz also needed a wife, so she sent Ruth to him. Ruth and Boaz liked each other and got married. Have each child pick up one pretzel stick to put with the others in his or her hand. **Now Naomi, Ruth, and Boaz were a very happy family.** Have the children count the sticks in their hands.

Later they had one bubbly, bouncing baby boy. Have each child add one more pretzel stick to his or her hand. **Now there were one, two, three, four people in Naomi's happy family.** Have the children count the sticks in their hands.

When this little boy grew up, he had more and more children. God blessed Naomi and Ruth because they chose to trust him.

Ask: • **When did Naomi and Ruth have to trust God?**

• **When do you trust God?**

Say: **Naomi and Ruth trusted God to take care of them when they were far away from their families and when they were sad. God gave them a new family, and everyone was happy again. We can trust God, just as Ruth and Naomi did.**

Samuel Listens to God

Are You Sleeping? •

cd1 track 27

Sing "Are You Sleeping?" to the tune of "Frère Jacques."

Are you sleeping? *(Lie down and pretend to sleep.)*
Are you sleeping,
Samuel? *(Continue to pretend to sleep.)*
Samuel?

Wake up, it is true. *(Open eyes.)*
God is calling you. *(Hold hand to ear.)*
Samuel. *(Stand up and turn around in place.)*
Samuel. *(Turn around in place.)*

Listen to God •

As you teach your children this finger play, remind them to listen to God.

Listen to God. What do you hear? *(Place hand behind ear and lean.)*

Listen to God. Use your ears. *(Point up.)*

Listen to God, like Samuel did. *(Place head on hands.)*

Listen to God. God speaks to kids. *(Point to others.)*

Samuel Listens to God •

1 Samuel 3

Bible Point: Listen to God.

Have your children make simple Samuel puppets out of standard-size envelopes. Before beginning, seal the empty envelopes, then cut the envelopes at the bottom, when held vertically, so the children's hands will slide up inside.

Give an envelope to each child, and let him or her make a simple sleeping face (a smile with closed eyes) on one side and a happy face (with eyes open) on the other side. Each child will also need a napkin.

Have the children begin by sliding their hands up into the envelopes with Samuel's sleeping face looking at them. Then help them place the napkins on their arms for Samuel's blanket. As you read the following Bible story rhyme, use a deep voice when God speaks and a higher voice for young Samuel.

Samuel, Samuel tucked in tight, sweetly dreaming in the night. *(Show sleeping Samuel.)*
  GOD: **Samuel! Samuel!**
  SAMUEL: **Here I am.** *(Show Samuel awake and raise arm. Blanket will fall off.)*
  Over to Eli Samuel ran. *(Eyes-open face moves toward other arm.)*
  SAMUEL: **You called me, sir.**
  ELI: **No I didn't. Go to bed.** *(Other hand points to Samuel.)*

Samuel, Samuel tucked in tight, sweetly dreaming in the night. *(Show sleeping Samuel.)*
  GOD: **Samuel! Samuel!**
  SAMUEL: **Here I am.** *(Show Samuel awake and raise arm. Blanket will fall off.)*
  Over to Eli Samuel ran. *(Eyes-open face moves toward other arm.)*
  SAMUEL: **You called me, sir.**

ELI: **No I didn't. Go to bed.** (*Other hand points to Samuel.*)

Samuel, Samuel tucked in tight, sweetly dreaming in the night. (*Show sleeping Samuel.*)

GOD: **Samuel! Samuel!**

SAMUEL: **Here I am.** (*Show Samuel awake and raise arm. Blanket will fall off.*)

Over to Eli Samuel ran. (*Eyes-open face moves toward other arm.*)

SAMUEL: **You called me, sir.**

ELI: **No I didn't. Go to bed.** (*Other hand points to Samuel.*) **Oh, wait, I know who you heard. The Lord called you.** (*Point finger at Samuel.*) **If one more time God calls, say to him, "Speak, and I will hear."** (*Place free hand behind your ear.*)

Samuel, Samuel tucked in tight, sweetly dreaming in the night. (*Show sleeping Samuel.*)

GOD: **Samuel! Samuel!**

SAMUEL: **Here I am.** (*Show Samuel awake and raise arm. Blanket will fall off.*)

The Lord came and stood by Samuel's bed. (*Wave hand over Samuel.*)

GOD: **Samuel! Samuel!**

SAMUEL: **Speak, Lord, I'll hear.** (*Cup hand to Samuel's "ear."*)

God spoke to Samuel very clear.

God spoke and Samuel heard. Samuel grew up with God's Word.

Ask: • **What are some ways we can hear God speak to us?**

Say: **We can listen to God when we go to church or when someone reads the Bible to us, and we're listening to God when we obey our parents. We can listen to God every day.**

David Becomes King

Who Will Be Our King?

cd1 track 28

Sing "Who Will Be Our King?" to the tune of "Skip to My Lou." Have the children stand up in a circle, holding hands. Choose a child to stand in the center of the circle, and place a crown on his or her head while the rest of the children circle around singing. At the end of the song, choose another "David" and sing again.

Who will be our king?
Who will be our king?

Who will be our king?
Our king will be [David]!

I Want the Crown

Your children will have fun taking turns standing, repeating the line below, and holding up the right amount of fingers during this fun finger play. Repeat the lines until you reach seven. Then have your shortest child be "brother number eight" and say David's lines. Remind the children that David had lots of brothers. Use a deep voice for the brothers.

CHILD: **I'm brother number one, and I want the crown.** (*Hold up one finger.*)

God didn't pick you. You sit down. (*Point down.*)

CHILD: **I'm brother number** [two]**, and I want the crown.** (*Hold up the correct number of fingers.*)

God didn't pick you. You sit down. (*Point down.*)

DAVID: **I'm brother number eight. I'm too young, right?** (*Hold up eight fingers.*)

DAVID: **But I love God with all my might.** (*Hug yourself.*)

Yes, David, you'll be the king one day. (*Pretend to place a crown on head.*)

You sing and love the Lord and pray. (*Show praying hands.*)

David Becomes a King

1 Samuel 16

Bible Point: God can use anyone.

Out of eight brothers, only one had a heart tall enough to be chosen as king over Israel…little David. Man looks on the outside, but God looks on the heart, as we should. God chose the youngest to be king. Children will enjoy this lesson since their small stature often leaves them feeling unimportant.

Before you begin, cut seven pictures of young men and one picture of a younger boy out of magazines for your children to hold up during the Bible story. Place a paper crown nearby. Have children practice the CHILDREN line before beginning. Ask the youngest child to hold youngest boy's picture.

Say: **It was Samuel's job to lead the people. The Lord said to Samuel, "I have chosen a new king. Go to the home of Jesse. He has eight sons. I'll show you which of his sons I have chosen to be the king."** Hold up the crown.

Samuel went to Jesse's house. He saw the first son. While this young man walked by (have a child hold up the first picture), **Samuel thought, "Wow! This young man must surely be the king. He is tall and handsome."**

CHILDREN: **No. God has not chosen him!**

Say: **God said, "He may be handsome, smart, and tall, but his love for me is just too small."**

A second young man walked by. Have a child hold up another picture. **Samuel thought, "This young man must surely be the king. He is tall and handsome."**

CHILDREN: **No. God has not chosen him!**

Say: **God said, "He may be handsome, smart, and tall, but his love for me is just too small."**

Another one of Jesse's sons walked by. Have a child hold up another picture. **Samuel thought, "This young man must surely be the king. He is tall and handsome."**

CHILDREN: **No. God has not chosen him!**

Say: **God said, "He may be handsome, smart, and tall, but his love for me is just too small."**

A fourth son of Jesse's walked by. Have a child hold up another picture. **Samuel thought, "This young man must surely be the king. He is tall and handsome."**

CHILDREN: **No. God has not chosen him!**

Say: **God said, "He may be handsome, smart, and tall, but his love for me is just too small."**

A fifth son of Jesse's walked by. Have a child hold up another picture. **Samuel thought, "This young man must surely be the king. He is tall and handsome."**

CHILDREN: **No. God has not chosen him!**

Say: **God said, "He may be handsome, smart, and tall, but his love for me is just too small."**

A sixth son of Jesse's walked by. Have a child hold up another picture. **Samuel thought, "This young man must surely be the king. He is tall and handsome."**

CHILDREN: **No. God has not chosen him!**

Say: **God said, "He may be handsome, smart, and tall, but his love for me is just too small."**

A seventh son of Jesse's walked by. Have a child hold up another picture. **Samuel thought, "This young man must surely be the king. He is tall and handsome."**

CHILDREN: **No. God has not chosen him!**

Say: **God said, "He may be handsome, smart, and tall, but his love for me is just too small."**

Samuel asked Jesse, "Are these all the sons you have?"

The father said, "Well, there is still the youngest boy. But he is little, and he is busy watching the sheep."

Samuel said, "Go and get him." Ask the child with the young boy's picture to stand up.

Samuel said, "Yes. This is David. He will be the king. He loves the Lord with all his heart." Put the crown on "David's" head, and then lead the children in clapping for the new king.

God can use anyone, big or small, young or old, short or tall.

Ask: • **How do you think God can use you?**

David Defeats Goliath

The Battle Is the Lord's

Invite your children to stand up in a circle. Lead them in marching as they sing "The Battle Is the Lord's" to the tune of "The Farmer in the Dell."

The battle is the Lord's.
The battle is the Lord's.

When there is something hard to do,
The battle is the Lord's.
(Repeat.)

Tall All Fall

Seat the children in a circle. Before you begin, whisper one of the adjectives to each child. Then go around the table describing Goliath. Repeat this group poem as often as the children like.

Goliath was mean, smelly, ugly, growly, tall,
    rude, nasty, loud, and strong.
David loved God and sang him songs. *(Sing this line.)*
Goliath was one, two, three, four, five, six,
    seven, eight, nine feet tall. *(Place fist over fist each time you say a number.)*

But to God, size doesn't matter at all.
David had one, two, three, four, five small
    stones. *(Hold up appropriate fingers.)*

With God's help, we're never alone. *(Wag finger.)*

One little rock flew, and down Goliath fell.
    (Bend over forward.)

Now that's a story we love to tell!

David Defeats Goliath

1 Samuel 16:11-12, 16; 17:1-51

Bible Point: God wants us to trust him.

Little, unknown David defeated huge, armored Goliath with only one stone. Your children will love to hear about David, the good guy, triumphing over the bad guy, Goliath. You will be helping your children feel braver as they learn that God can work through small people, like them, to defeat big problems.

Before you begin, collect a variety of boxes. As you tell the story, stack the boxes. Draw Goliath's mean face on a piece of paper, and tape it to the top box. Your children will delight in knocking down their giant.

Say: **There was a war going on when David was a boy. The bad Philistines who didn't worship God wanted to fight God's people, the Israelites who loved God. Goliath was a Philistine and a** *big, bad* **giant! He was one, two, three, four, five, six, seven, eight, nine feet tall!** Invite the children to count along with you. **Goliath was mean.**

Ask: • **Who's the meanest person that you know of on TV?**

Say: **Goliath was probably just as mean. He wore a strong helmet** (have kids touch their heads) **and a coat of armor all over his body.** Have kids stroke each arm one at a time. **Even his legs carried heavy iron to protect him. Goliath had a huge, pointy spear and a sharp, bladed sword.** Have the children pretend to wave a sword. **His shield was bigger than you. The Bible says that Goliath was so scary that even the bravest soldiers in Israel ran away and hid from him.**

Now David was the baby boy in his family. He had seven older brothers. He was the smallest one in his family.

Ask: • **Who is the smallest person in your family?**

Say: **Little David's job was to watch the sheep for his family. He cuddled the mama sheep and let the little lambs lick milk off his finger.** Lead the children in stroking the backs of their hands, pretending to pet a lamb. **David loved to sing and make music for God while he was watching the sheep. He would lie under the trees in the field and pray to God while the lambs played at his feet. David trusted God.**

Now the giant Goliath wanted to fight someone. He stood on his hill and shouted in his deep, scary, growly voice, "Choose a man to fight me! Come on. Just try to get me!"

The Israelites only shook with fear and ran to hide, but not David. David said, "You come against me with your sword and spear. But with God there is nothing to fear." David picked up one, two, three, four, five smooth stones. He put one in his sling and swung it around and around. David shot the rock, and it flew through the air. It hit that giant Goliath right in the middle of his forehead! And boom, Goliath fell facedown on the ground. Everybody cheered for little David, who won the battle that day between the Philistines and the Israelites. David trusted God that day, just as God wants us to trust him.

Ask: • **How did David show that he trusted God?**

• **What "giant" things make you feel afraid?**

• **What are some ways you can trust God?**

Say: **David was brave and trusted God. When you feel afraid, you can pray, and God will help you trust him too.**

David and Jonathan Are Friends

Two Good Friends
cd1 track 30

Sing "Two Good Friends" to the tune of "Three Blind Mice." Direct the children to stand up while they sing.

Two good friends. Two good friends. *(Hold up two fingers spread apart.)*

They stick together. They stick together. *(Bring fingers together.)*

They stick together from head to toe. *(Touch head, then toes.)*

They stick together through high and low. *(Reach hands up high, then bring them down.)*

They stick together through yes and no. *(Nod "yes," then shake head "no.")*

Two good friends. *(Hold up two fingers.)*

Friends to the End

Help each child find a partner, and have partners sit on the floor and face each other. Tell them that they are friends like Jonathan and David. Instruct them to begin the finger play with both of their hands behind their backs.

Jonathan loved God. David loved God. *(Hold up one index finger, then hold up the other index finger.)*

Jonathan trusted God. David trusted God. *(Point up with the one index finger, then with the other index finger.)*

Jonathan fought the Philistines. David fought the Philistines. *(Wiggle one index finger as if it were a sword, then wiggle the other index finger.)*

Jonathan had a big heart, and David had a big heart. *(Make a big heart in the air with fingers, then make a heart on chest.)*

I love God, and so does my friend. Our friendship will never end. *(Shake hands with partner.)*

Have the partners take turns telling each other one or two things they like, such as jumping in puddles or eating an ice cream.

David and Jonathan Are Friends

1 Samuel 18:1-4, 19:1-7, 20:1-42

Bible Point: We can trust God.

Jonathan and David stayed faithful friends despite the wish of Jonathan's father, King Saul, to have David killed. Jonathan knew that while David was alive, Jonathan would never inherit the throne, but that never deterred his devotion to David. Their loyalty is a beautiful example of real friendship and trust in God.

Before you begin, cut out a small crown for each child from yellow construction paper, and cut a circular rock-shape out of brown construction paper for each child. Have children sit in a circle on the floor or at a table.

Set out crayons, the crowns, and the rocks. Give each child three Styrofoam cups. Instruct kids to turn the Styrofoam cups upside down and make three puppets by drawing the following simple faces on the front: *mean* king Saul, *nice* Jonathan, and *nice* David. Have the children tape the yellow crown to King Saul, line their puppets up in front of them, and follow the actions of your puppets as you tell the Bible story. You will also need three toothpicks for spears during the Bible story.

Say: **Jonathan was the son of King Saul.** Move "Jonathan" out in front of the other puppets. Lift up "King Saul," then place him back down. **He liked being friends with David** (move "David" next to Jonathan), **and David liked being friends with Jonathan. Jonathan even gave David his special robe and his sword.** Move the puppets back into line. Then move King Saul forward.

King Saul grew jealous and began to hate David.

Hold up King Saul, tilt him back and forth, and lead the children in saying the following line in an angry voice: **I don't like David! David must go!** Then set him back down.

Hold up Jonathan, tilt him back and forth, and lead the children in saying the following line in a calm voice: **But David is my friend.** Then set him back down.

Hold up King Saul, tilt him back and forth, and lead the children in saying the following line in an angry voice: **As long as David is alive, people will want *him* as king. I'm going to get rid of him.** Then set him back down.

Say: **So King Saul threw a spear at David, but it missed, and David got away.** Have the children watch as you throw a toothpick from King Saul past David. **David trusted God, and God protected him. David went into a field and hid behind a rock so King Saul couldn't find him.** Bring David out front, and lean the brown rock in front of David. **Jonathan knew where David was, and Jonathan wanted to help his friend.**

Ask: • **What would you do to help your friend?**

Say: **Jonathan went to find out if King Saul was still angry with David.**

Hold up King Saul, tilt him back and forth, and lead the children in saying the following line in an angry voice: **Where is David? I want to get rid of him!** Then set him back down.

Say: **Jonathan wouldn't tell where David was hiding. King Saul was so angry with Jonathan that he threw his spear at him!** Have the children watch as you throw a toothpick from King Saul past Jonathan. **But it *missed* also! God protected Jonathan.**

Jonathan snuck out of the palace to warn David that it was too dangerous to come back home. Move Jonathan toward David. **Jonathan shot three arrows past the rock where David was hiding.** Lead the children in counting to three as you toss three toothpicks past David.

The arrows were a signal that King Saul was still angry. David needed to run away and not come back until King Saul had calmed down.

David came out from behind the rock. Set the rock aside. **David bowed three times to Jonathan because he was the prince. They cried because they knew that David would stay away a long time.** Pick up David and count to three as he bows toward Jonathan. Move David and Jonathan close to each other, then pretend to cry and say goodbye. **They promised to be friends forever!**

God kept David safe for many years. When King Saul died, the crown didn't go to Jonathan, King Saul's son. It went to David. Move the crown from King Saul's head to David's. Then hold King David up. **David became the new king. King David loved God and served the people well. David and Jonathan trusted God, and God took care of them all their lives.**

Ask: • **Who are some people you trust?**

• **What are some ways we show God that we trust him?**

Say: **One way we show God that we trust him is to pray and listen to what he says through the Bible. David and Jonathan loved God, trusted each other, and trusted God to keep David safe. We can trust God too.**

Toothpicks tend to be sharp. To avoid children poking each other with the ends, you can break the points ahead of time or put the toothpicks away immediately after use.

Solomon Asks for Wisdom

Ask God for Wisdom

Sing "Ask God for Wisdom" to the tune of "Pop Goes the Weasel."

God will teach us if we just ask *(fold hands and bow head in prayer)*

The things we need to know to *(point to side of head)*

Make good choices every day. *(Stretch arms out wide.)*

Ask God for wisdom! *(Jump up with hands stretched up in the air.)*

Be Wise

Solomon obeyed God and followed his rules. God told Solomon he would reward him with wisdom, riches, and a long life if he would walk in his ways, obey God, and do what's right.

God teaches us to do what's right *(point up, then give thumbs up)*

In the morning *(stretch arms up as if waking up),*

Noon *(make a circle with arms above head),*

And night. *(Lay head on hands.)*

Solomon Asks for Wisdom

1 Kings 2:1-4; 3:3-28

Bible Point: God wants to give us wisdom.

When God asked Solomon what he wanted, Solomon asked for wisdom to lead and rule God's people. This request pleased God; God told Solomon that he would give him wisdom as well as bless him with riches and a long life. God told Solomon to walk in his ways and obey his laws and Solomon would be blessed.

As you teach your children about Solomon, you'll also help them learn to obey God.

Children will enjoy acting out this rhyming story. Lead your children in doing the motions as you read the following Bible story.

Solomon was the king *(make a circle with hands, and place them on head)*
And ruled with God in mind *(tap side of head),*
Obeyed God's rules and laws *(point up),*
Was fair and good and kind.

Once while Solomon slept *(rest head on hands),*
God asked him in a dream,
"Solomon, what do you want? *(Hold hands up and shrug shoulders.)*

I'll give you anything." *(Bring hands forward with palms up.)*

Solomon asked for wisdom *(tap side of head)*
To be smart and, oh, so wise.
He asked to be a good king *(make a circle with hands, and place them on head)*
And always know what's right. *(Show thumbs up.)*

God was pleased with Solomon *(smile big and point to mouth)*

For his unselfish plea. *(Bring hands forward, palms up.)*

God said, "You'll get your wisdom. *(Tap side of head.)*

And much more than that, you'll see." *(Spread hands out, palms up.)*

Solomon ruled God's people *(make a circle with hands, and place them on head)*

And showed them what was right. *(Show thumbs up.)*

He taught them to do good
And please God in his sight. *(Point up.)*

When two women came *(stand up and show two fingers)*

And argued, fought, and fussed *(place hands on hips and stomp feet)*,

Solomon used the wisdom *(tap side of head)*
God gave him to be just.

Solomon knew the answer. *(Tap side of head.)*
He knew which woman lied. *(Wag fingers.)*
He gave the mom the baby. *(Pretend to rock a baby.)*
"She's the one!" he cried. *(Point to a friend.)*

The people were amazed *(show a surprised look)*
At what Solomon would do. *(Point up.)*
They knew he was of God,
They knew it through and through. *(Show thumbs up.)*

Obey God's rules and laws *(point up)*,
And you'll be richly blessed.
Obey God's rules and laws *(point up)*—
That was Solomon's test.

Ask: • **What do you think makes a person wise?**
• **Who do you know who is smart?**
• **What are some ways God can give you wisdom?**
Say: **God wants to give us all wisdom if we ask him. We become wise through talking to God and listening to him. And we can become wise through listening to God's Word, the Bible, when someone reads it to us. God wants to give us wisdom.**

Elijah Helps a Widow

God Cares for Us

Have your children stand up in a circle and sing "God Cares for Us" to the tune of "When the Saints Go Marching In."

A drop of oil, a little meal (*pretend to eat*),
A drop of oil, a little meal (*pretend to eat*)
Made some bread to feed Elijah. (*Turn and pretend to feed the person next to you.*)
God was sure to care for him! (*Give a high five.*)

That drop of oil, that little meal (*pretend to eat*),
That drop of oil, that little meal (*pretend to eat.*)
Never ran out for Elijah. (*Turn and pretend to feed the person next to you.*)
God was sure to care for him! (*Give a high five.*)

God cares for us. God cares for us. (*Give a high five with one hand, then with the other.*)
Our God will always care for us! (*Give a high five.*)
God took good care of Elijah.
God will always care for us! (*Hug yourself.*)

Here Is Elijah

God took care of Elijah's needs, the widow's needs, and her son's needs. As you teach your children about Elijah, remind them that God will take care of our needs, too. Have the children start with their hands behind their backs.

Here is Elijah. His tummy is hungry, and his mouth is so dry. (*Hold up and wiggle index finger.*)

Here is Elijah. He looks to the sky. (*Point up, then put hands behind back.*)

Here is the widow. Her tummy is hungry, and her mouth is so dry. (*Hold up and wiggle index finger.*)

Here is the son. She thinks they'll both die. (*Continue holding up index finger, then hold up little finger of opposite hand. Bring both hands behind back.*)

Here is Elijah. "Make me a cake—please, go." (*Hold up and wiggle index finger.*)

Here is Elijah. "Your flour and oil are sure to overflow." (*Bring hands toward each other, up, then out like a fountain. Then place hands behind back.*)

Here is the son, who gets very sick. (*Hold up and wiggle little finger.*)

Here is the widow. "Please heal my son quick!" (*Hold up and wiggle index finger, then put hands behind back.*)

Here is Elijah. He makes the boy well. *(Hold up and wiggle opposite index finger.)*

And everyone is glad! His story we'll tell! *(Hold up all fingers and wiggle them.)*

God is in heaven. This story is true. *(Hold up index finger.)*

God is in heaven. He'll take care of you! *(Hold up index finger, then hug yourself.)*

Elijah Helps a Widow

1 Kings 17:7-24

Bible Point: God will take care of you.

God used a widow to help care for Elijah. In turn, Elijah helped her receive God's care.

Before you begin, place about a tablespoon of flour in a gallon-size resealable bag and about a tablespoon of oil in a clear, plastic bottle. Place about two cups of flour in a bowl, and set that aside with a large tablespoon. Then set aside a measuring cup of oil and a funnel. Invite the children to join you and sit in a circle.

Say: **Elijah was one of God's prophets. God used him to tell other people things God wanted them to know.**

A famine came over the land. No food could grow, and all water in the rivers dried up. God told Elijah to go find a certain widow and she would take care of him. When he found the woman, he asked her for food. She told him she only had a little bit of flour (hold up the bag with the small amount of flour) **and a little bit of oil.** (Hold up the bottle containing a small amount of oil.) **"Surely my son and I will starve," the widow said. "I have nothing I can give you."**

"You will not starve," said Elijah. "God will take care of you."

Have each child pass the bag of flour to the person sitting next to him or her and say, "God will take care of you."

Say: **Elijah told the woman to make a loaf of bread with the oil and flour for him first and God would take care of her and her son's needs. "Your flour and oil will not be used up until it rains again." How could that be? But she believed Elijah and made the first loaf of bread for him.**

Pass the bowl of flour, spoon, and resealable bag of flour. Let each child add a spoonful of flour from the bowl to the bag. Using the funnel, add oil to fill the bottle for the children to see.

Ask: • **What do you think happened after the widow made the bread for Elijah?**

Say: **It happened just as Elijah had said! The widow never ran out of flour and oil! They never went hungry, and God took care of them.**

Some time later, the widow's son became very sick and stopped breathing. The boy never woke up. But God was still taking care of the widow and her son, so he told Elijah to save the boy. Choose one child to lie down in the center of the circle. Let each of the children take turns folding their hands as if praying and saying, "God will take care of you." After everyone who wants to has had a turn, have the child sit up.

Elijah prayed and asked God to bring the boy back to life, and God did it.

Ask: • **How did God take care of Elijah? the widow and her son?**

• **Why do you think God took care of the widow and her son?**

• **Why does God take care of you?**

Say: **God took care of Elijah, the widow, and her son because he loved them. God takes care of you, too, because he loves you.**

Elijah Challenges the Prophets of Baal

Hands Down!

Play this fun rap, and let your children hit musical sticks together or use noisemakers to the rhythm of the beat.

Elijah was a man of God.
When God said, "Go," Elijah would nod.
God sent Elijah to an evil king
To show him God's more powerful than anything!

Let us shout an' let us sing:
GOD'S MORE POWERFUL THAN ANYTHING!
There's no problem when God's around
'Cause God will win [clap, clap] HANDS DOWN!

King Ahab, you're a wicked king!
You worship gods that don't mean a thing!
There's gonna be a big showdown,
But God will win [clap, clap] HANDS DOWN!

Let us shout an' let us sing:
GOD'S MORE POWERFUL THAN ANYTHING!
There's no problem when God's around
'Cause God will win [clap, clap] HANDS DOWN!

So they built an altar of stone and mud,
But Ahab's god was just a dud!
There wasn't a spark of flame around!
Now God would win [clap, clap] HANDS DOWN!

Let us shout an' let us sing:
GOD'S MORE POWERFUL THAN ANYTHING!
There's no problem when God's around
'Cause God will win [clap, clap] HANDS DOWN!

Then God sent a fiery flash of flame,
And the people shouted, "GOD'S HIS NAME!"
They bowed their faces to the ground!
And God had won [clap, clap] HANDS DOWN!

Let us shout an' let us sing:
GOD'S MORE POWERFUL THAN ANYTHING!
There's no problem when God's around
'Cause God will win [clap, clap] HANDS DOWN!

There's Only One God

Elijah felt all alone in his faith in God. Baal's worshippers were many. Elijah proved to Baal's followers that Baal did not exist. Elijah showed the people that there is only one true God.

Here are Baal's followers; they don't believe in God. *(Hold up one hand and wiggle fingers.)*

Here is Elijah; he believes in God. *(Hold up and wiggle index finger on other hand.)*

Baal's followers yell, "Where are you, Baal?" *(Hold up and wiggle five fingers.)*

There's no answer—there *is* no Baal! *(Shrug shoulders.)*

Elijah calls on God, "God, are you there?" *(Hold up and wiggle index finger on other hand.)*

God starts a mighty fire—there's only one God!
Now *all* the people believe there's only one God! *(Hold up and wiggle all ten fingers.)*

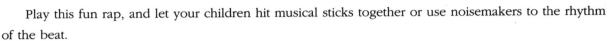

Elijah and the Prophets of Baal

1 Kings 18:16-40

Bible Point: Our God is the only true god.

Elijah sought to prove that the Lord God was the only true God. He wanted Baal's followers to know that Baal was false and untrue. He did this in an amazing fashion, by calling on God to light a drenched altar. Your children will begin to believe that there is only one true God as they help you re-create this story.

Before you begin, set out wooden blocks, red and blue tissue paper, and a roll of red crepe paper.

Say: **Elijah was a prophet of God. That meant that God used Elijah to tell people special things that God wanted them to know. During Elijah's days, many people worshipped a false god that they called Baal. They believed Baal could do things that he really couldn't, so God wanted Elijah to show the people just how wrong they were.**

Elijah dared Baal's followers to see who was the one and only true god—Elijah's God or Baal. Elijah told the followers of Baal to build an altar. Altars were made of large rocks stacked up in a pile and were used to burn sacrifices and worship gods. The people built an altar to Baal, then called on Baal to light the fire on the altar.

Let your children work together to stack the wooden blocks in a pile.

Say: **Baal didn't answer the people, and no fire came down to light the altar.**

Ask: • **Hmm. Why do you think Baal didn't send down fire to light the altar?**

Say: **Now it was Elijah's turn. He built an altar**

too. Let the children stack up wooden blocks to make a second altar.

Elijah knew God could send down fire to burn the sacrifice, so he asked people to pour water all over the altar so the fire couldn't burn. Let children tear blue tissue paper and place it around the wood.

Even though the altar was soaking wet, Elijah knew that God could burn it up anyway. It was Elijah's turn now to call out to God, "God, please start a fire on the altar." Have children stand up and circle around the altar with praying hands and say, "God, please send your fire."

Ask: • **What do you think happened?**

Say: **A fire came down right away and burned up the sacrifice and even all the water that was poured all around.** Let children tear red tissue paper into strips and toss them all over the altar.

The people were so amazed that they fell to the ground. Encourage children to dramatically, but carefully, fall to the ground. **Then the people really believed in God!** Have children stand up, give them each about a three-foot streamer of red crepe paper, and let them jump and skip around the altar, waving their streamers and chanting, "There is only one God! There is only one God!"

Ask: • **Was Baal a real god? Why or why not?**

• **How did Elijah show that his God was the one and only true God?**

• **Which god do you want to believe in—God or Baal?**

Say: **God wants us to know that he is the one and only true God.**

Use less blue paper than red so that the "fire" covers up the "water" when re-creating the Bible story.

Elisha Helps a Widow and Her Sons

God Will Take Good Care of You

cd1 track 34

Sing "God Will Take Good Care of You" to the tune of "Mary Had a Little Lamb."

God will take good care of you *(point up)*,
Care of you *(point to someone else)*,
Care of you. *(Point to someone else.)*
God will take good care of you. *(Point up.)*
The Bible says it's true. *(Hold hands in front of you like a book.)*

God will take good care of me *(point up, then hug yourself)*,
Care of me *(hug yourself)*,
Care of me. *(Hug yourself.)*
God will take good care of me. *(Point up, then hug yourself.)*
This I do believe. *(Tap side of head.)*

The Widow and Her Boys

Elisha helps a widow who is about to lose her sons to creditors. He reminds the woman that God will take care of her and her sons. Remind your children often that God will take care of them, just like he loves and takes care of all his creations.

God will take care of you—widow and sons.
(Pretend to pat little heads.)

God will take care of you; look at the dawn.
(Open and wiggle fingers in front of face like a starburst.)

God will take care of you, just like the fawns.
(Place fingers open on top of head like antlers.)

God will take care of you, so just lie down and yawn. *(Rest head on hands.)*

Tip From the Trenches

Before you begin, explain to children that the dawn is early in the morning when the sun bursts into the sky. Let them know, also, that a fawn is a baby deer.

Elisha Helps a Widow and Her Sons

2 Kings 4:1-7

Bible Point: God will take care of you.

A widow approached Elisha and asked for his help. Because the widow had no husband and no money, creditors were about to take her sons from her to use as slaves. Elisha the prophet revealed to her what she must do. She did not hesitate but followed Elisha's words in faith and obedience to God. As you share this lesson with your children, remind them that we can have faith that God will take care of us, too.

Before you begin, hide a clear plastic cup for each of your children somewhere in the classroom. Save one cup to show the children. Set aside a pitcher with enough water to fill each of the cups halfway.

Say: **Way back in Bible days, there lived a woman with two sons. The woman was a widow. That means that her husband had died. She had no one to work and make money for her family. She didn't have food to eat. Some of the people to whom the widow owed money wanted to take away her sons as payment for her bills.**

Ask: • **How would you feel if you were going to be taken away from your mom or dad?**

• **How do you think the sons might have felt?**

Say: **The widow had faith that God would take care of her. She had faith that God would not allow her sons to be taken from her.**

The widow asked Elisha, one of God's prophets, for help. Elisha told the widow, "Go to all of your neighbors, and ask them to let you borrow all of their empty jars. Borrow lots and lots of jars."

Let's pretend to go to our neighbors' houses and ask for jars. Show the children one of the cups so they know what to look for. Have each child hunt for one cup and then come back and sit down in the circle. When all the children have found cups and are sitting down, continue the story.

Elisha told her to go home with the jars *and* her sons, then close the doors. Let's pretend to do that. Walk to a table with the children, closing a door if one is available.

Then Elisha told her to pour oil into the jars. She kept pouring and pouring, and her oil was never used up! God gave her lots and lots of extra oil! Every empty jar was now filled to the top with oil! Let's pretend to do that. We won't use oil because it could be messy, but we'll use water to fill all of your cups. Pour water into each child's cup, filling halfway.

Elisha told the woman to sell the oil and use the money to pay the people to whom she owed money.

The widow was so happy! God took care of the widow and her sons, and God will take care of you. Have children say, "God takes care of me," and then drink the water from their cups.

Ask: • **How did God take care of the widow and her sons?**

• **What are some ways God takes care of you?**

God Heals Naaman

Who's That Washing?

Sing "Who's That Washing?" to the tune of "Clementine."

Who's that washing in the river (*pretend to wash arms*),
In the Jordan's muddy tide? (*Make a disgusted face.*)
It's the mighty captain Naaman (*salute*),
Humbling his foolish pride. (*Fold hands and bow.*)

Who's that dipping seven times (*hold up seven fingers and squat down*),
Like the prophet said to do? (*Stand up and squat down.*)
It's the mighty captain Naaman (*stand and salute*)—
Now his skin looks all brand new! (*Rub cheeks and smile.*)

Naaman Had Some Spots

When Naaman chose to obey God, his leprosy was healed. Have fun with this counting finger play as you reinforce the point: "Obeying God is best." Each time you count, hold up the same amount of fingers as you say.

One, two, three, four, five, six, seven...
Naaman had white spots.
Naaman had white sores.

One, two, three, four, five, six, seven...
He wanted to be healed.
He wanted to get well.

One, two, three, four, five, six, seven...
Elisha said to Naaman, "Wash in the river."
Elisha said to Naaman, "Dip yourself seven times."

One, two, three, four, five, six, seven...
Hurray! The spots are gone!
Hurray! The spots are gone!

One, two, three, four, five, six, seven...
He trusted and believed in God.
Naaman praised the Lord.

God Heals Naaman

2 Kings 5:1-16

Bible Point: Obeying God is best.

Naaman was in charge of the army for the king of Aram. Though a great soldier, he was troubled with leprosy. When the prophet Elisha gave Naaman an unusual task to heal his leprosy, Naaman didn't want to do it. But when Naaman obeyed the prophet, his leprosy was healed. As you teach your children about Naaman, remind them that it may not always be easy to obey God, but it is always what is best!

Before you begin, gather a CD player, an upbeat children's praise CD, a garbage can, and about ten white stickers for each of your children. Sheets of stationery-type stickers work great!

Say: **Leprosy is a disease that some people had during the Bible days. It looks kind of like white spots all over your skin. There was no medicine that could take it away either. Once you got leprosy, you had it for the rest of your life. Let's play a game and pretend to be the man in our Bible story that has leprosy.**

Give each of your children about ten white stickers. Tell them they will play a Tag-type game. When they hear the music, they are to place all of their stickers on their classmates' arms before the music stops. Say, "Go!" and begin the CD. Encourage the children to hurry before the music stops. Stop the CD when you see that the last stickers are being placed. Gather the children back in a circle on the floor and continue.

Say: **In our Bible story, there was an important man who had leprosy. He didn't know God, but God loved him just the same. His name was Naaman. He was a great army leader and a rich man with lots of servants.**

Naaman's wife had a servant girl who obeyed God and believed in him. One day the servant girl told Naaman about the prophet Elisha who could heal his leprosy. *Oh,* **Naaman liked that! Naaman wanted to be healed! "Could that be** *possible***?" he thought. So he went to this prophet Elisha hoping to be healed.**

He walked up to the door. Have the children stand up and walk in place. **He knocked.** Have the children pretend to knock on the door and make a clacking sound with their tongues. **He told the servant that he wanted to speak to Elisha about being healed of his leprosy. When the servant came back, he didn't bring Elisha with him, as Naaman had**

expected. **He just told Naaman that Elisha said to go wash in the Jordan River seven times.**

Now, Naaman was an important man. "This man Elisha should have come and told me in person. Doesn't he know how important I am? And wash in the muddy Jordan River? He's a crazy man! No way!" He didn't want to obey the prophet. He didn't want to obey God's Word. But Naaman's servants reminded him how badly he wanted to be healed and that the mud wouldn't hurt him. "So why not give it a try?" they said. Naaman finally agreed and traveled on until they came to the Jordan River.

Let's pretend to get out of our chariot, take off our coat, and begin to get into the muddy Jordan River.

Be overly dramatic, and lead your children in acting out getting out of a chariot, taking off a coat, and getting into the muddy water of the Jordan River.

Say: **Now, Naaman thought that this was a silly way to be healed. At first, he just said, "Humpfff! This isn't going to heal me!" But Naaman really wanted to be healed, so he decided to obey.**

Let's pretend to dip down in the water seven times. Each time we come up out of the water, take a few stickers off. When we say, "seven," all the spots should be gone. One, two, three, four, five, six, seven. Lead the children in counting and taking off their spots.

Look! The leprosy is gone! God healed Naaman! When Naaman obeyed God, God healed his leprosy! We can obey God too. As you bring me your stickers for the garbage can, I'd like for you to say, "We can obey God." Have each of the children drop their stickers in the garbage and say, "We can obey God."

Jehoshaphat Trusts God for Victory

Oh, Do You Know?

cd1 track 36

Have your children stand up and sing "Oh, Do You Know?" to the tune of "The Muffin Man."

Oh, do you know Jehoshaphat *(pretend to ask other class friends)*,
Jehoshaphat, Jehoshaphat?
Oh, do you know Jehoshaphat,
Who felt very afraid? *(Shake as if afraid.)*

What can you do, Jehoshaphat *(shrug shoulders),*
Jehoshaphat, Jehoshaphat?
What can you do, Jehoshaphat?
You can pray and pray. *(Make praying hands.)*

When you pray, Jehoshaphat *(kneel down),*
Jehoshaphat, Jehoshaphat;
When you pray, Jehoshaphat,
God will make you safe. *(Hug yourself.)*

You can trust God, Jehoshaphat *(point up),*
Jehoshaphat, Jehoshaphat.
You can trust God, Jehoshaphat,
Because God cares for you. *(Hug a friend.)*

Judah Is Victorious

King Jehoshaphat's people were coming under attack by several nearby armies. Though Judah was outnumbered, King Jehoshaphat trusted God to protect his people. Using your fingers, help your children experience that God is always victorious, no matter what the circumstances.

There once was a king named Jehoshaphat,
  who trusted in God above. *(Point up.)*

There once was a group of soldiers who put on
  their fighting hats. *(Put hands on head as if wearing a hat.)*

The king of Judah, Jehoshaphat, bowed and
  then prayed. *(Make praying hands.)*

While all of Judah slept, the armies fought and
  hit. *(Rest head on hands as if sleeping.)*

Now the army men were gone, but Judah was
  well and fit! *(Make strong arms.)*

Jehoshaphat Trusts God for Victory

2 Chronicles 20:1-30

Bible Point: We can trust God.

King Jehoshaphat loved God. He trusted God to take care of him. When King Jehoshaphat learned that several armies were about to attack his kingdom, he trusted God to be victorious. As your children help retell this story, teach them that they can trust God too.

Before you begin, set out wooden blocks.

Say: **Jehoshaphat was the king of Judah. He was a good king and trusted in God. He knew that God took care of him, and he trusted God to protect and take care of his people, too.**

One day, some men told King Jehoshaphat that some armies wanted to attack Jehoshaphat's kingdom and hurt all of the people. Jehoshaphat immediately prayed to God, asking God for help, because Jehoshaphat knew that he could trust God.

Ask: • **What kinds of things do you pray about?**

Say: **King Jehoshaphat gathered his army of men. He knew that he had a smaller army and that there were lots and lots of men in the other armies. Let's see just how many men there were.**

Have the children stand the wooden blocks on end. Tell them that these are all the other army men that want to fight King Jehoshaphat and his army.

Say: **The night before the battle, Jehoshaphat and all the people of Judah stood before God and**

prayed. Have the children stand up, bow their heads, and pretend to pray. Then have them sit down. **They worshipped God and asked him for protection. The people of Judah trusted God to take care of them.**

While the people of Judah were still sleeping, God allowed the armies to begin fighting. The other armies got confused and fought each *other* instead of Jehoshaphat's men, whom they were supposed to be fighting. Have the children knock down all the blocks.

Early in the morning, Jehoshaphat and his army began to climb the hill. Let's pretend to climb. Move arms and legs as if climbing.

When the army got to the other side, all they could see were bodies lying on the ground. Put one hand over your eyes and look toward the blocks. **The people praised God and thanked him for their victory! Jehoshaphat's people trusted God, and God took care of the people of Judah without them even fighting!**

Ask: • **What are some ways God takes care of you?**

• **How do you trust God?**

Say: **God takes care of us every day by providing food for us to eat. Each time we sit down to eat, we trust that God will satisfy our tummies and make us feel full. We can trust God every day!**

Tip From the Trenches

Use many wooden blocks to represent the armies of men. Show the children how uneven the sides were, pointing out how amazing Jehoshaphat's victory really was.

Josiah Finds God's Word

Read God's Word

cd1 track 37

Have the children stand as you lead them in singing and doing the motions to "Read God's Word" to the tune of "The Mulberry Bush."

Find someone to read God's Word (*pretend to open a book*),
Read God's Word, read God's Word.
Find someone to read God's Word
Each and every day.

Listen and obey God's Word (*place hand behind ear*),
Obey God's Word, obey God's Word.
Listen and obey God's Word
Each and every day.

Clean the Temple

Remind the children through this finger play that we need to take care of our church and that we need to pay attention to God's Word.

Here is the church. (*Make a triangle with hands, fingertips touching.*)

There's nobody there. (*Look through the triangular hole.*)

Here is the church. (*Make a triangle with hands, fingertips touching.*)

It needs some repair. (*Turn hands all around, looking at the "church" from all angles.*)

Open the door and go in to clean. (*Fold hands open, vertically like a door.*)

Now it looks better—see what I mean? (*Turn hands all around, looking at the "church" from all angles.*)

Look—over there. What do I see? (*Look through the triangular hole.*)

It's God's holy Word, for you and me! (*Open hands horizontally like a book, and move forward.*)

Josiah Finds God's Word

2 Chronicles 34

Bible Point: Remember to worship God.

In Josiah's day, many people had abandoned God. Though just a young lad, King Josiah tried to remove all the false gods and idols throughout Israel. In repairing and cleaning the Temple, Josiah's men found the Book of the Law, God's Word. Josiah knew and understood the importance of God's Word. As children are allowed to touch and see God's Word, the Bible, you will be planting and cultivating a love for God in each of your children's hearts.

Before you begin, put a ribbon or bow on the front of a Bible. Hide the Bible in the room, out of sight of all the children. Set up small towers of blocks around the room.

Ask: • **How old do you think most kings are?**

Say: **The king in our Bible story today was only eight years old when he became king. Can you imagine being eight years old and being the king?**

Ask: • **How would you feel if you were king or queen of an entire country?**

• **What would you do?**

Say: **King Josiah was a very wise boy. Even though he was very young, he knew how important it was to worship God and obey God.**

Many people during Josiah's day had forgotten all about God and didn't care about worshipping him. But it was important to King Josiah. He wanted to worship God. He knew how important God's rules and laws were, and he wanted everyone to want to worship God.

One day he had his men tear down all the altars in the land that were built to worship all the false gods. He ordered the false statues and images be broken and destroyed. Josiah had his men begin to clean God's Temple so they could worship him again. Let's clean up this room like Josiah cleaned up Israel. Direct children to knock down all the towers you set up before this activity and then put the blocks away.

Ask: • **How would you feel if your parents didn't want to bring you to church?**

• **How would you feel if you came to a dirty church every week?**

• **What do you think might happen if everyone forgot to come to church and worship God?**

Say: **The Temple had gotten into such a mess that it needed to be cleaned and rebuilt. While they were cleaning, the workers found something very, very important that had been missing for a long time.**

Let's have a hunt in our classroom to find that something special. You'll know it's what we're looking for because it will have a big bow on the front. Let your children find the hidden Bible and then return to their seats.

Wonderful! Look what you've found! It's God's Word, the Bible! The people had forgotten about God for such a long time that they didn't even know where his book of laws was!

Josiah was so happy to find God's Word that he had it read aloud to him. He made everyone promise to obey God's Word and to listen to God.

Ask: • **How did you feel when you found God's Word?**

• **What are some ways you can worship God?**

• **Who can you ask to read God's Word to you this week?**

Say: **God wants us to learn about him and worship him by listening to or reading the Bible, praying, and coming to church. Remember to worship God this week.**

Tip From the Trenches

If you have a large group, section the room with masking tape and hide a Bible in each section. Form small groups of children, and have each group find a Bible.

Nehemiah Rebuilds the Wall

This Is the Way We Build

track 1

Sing "This Is the Way We Build" to the tune of "The Mulberry Bush."

This is the way we build the wall (*pound fist over fist*),
Build the wall, build the wall.
This is the way we build the wall
Around Jerusalem! (*Stretch out arms while turning in a circle.*)

This is the way we stack the stones (*pretend to stack stones*),
Stack the stones, stack the stones.
This is the way we build the wall
Around Jerusalem! (*Stretch out arms while turning in a circle.*)

Building the Wall

Have your children join you and sit down in a circle. Teach this finger play to your children to help them learn that God helps us do big things for him, even when we think the job is too big for us.

Brick by brick. Brick by brick. (*Pound fists one over the other.*)

Build a wall, brick by brick.
Mean people said, "No! You cannot build this wall. (*Wag a finger "no."*)

You can try all you want; it's only going to fall." (*Bring hands down to the ground.*)

The people were sad. "Maybe we should quit." (*Let hands droop from the wrists.*)
Nehemiah said, "Wait! God can handle it." (*Smile a big smile.*)

Brick by brick. Brick by brick. (*Pound fists one over the other.*)

Build a wall, brick by brick.

Nehemiah Rebuilds the Wall

Nehemiah 2:11–6:19

Bible Point: God can use you.

Nehemiah led his people in rebuilding the walls of their capital city. Enemy armies had torn down the walls so that the enemy could get in and out. The wall around the city was broken and burned. Only Nehemiah believed that God could use him and his people to fix the walls. As you teach this story, you are helping build the belief in your children's hearts that God can use us to do big things.

Begin by having your children build a wall out of LEGO building blocks or other items that will stack. Tell your children that they are being important helpers and that the wall will be used to tell the Bible story. Prepare them for the wall to be broken so they won't be upset later.

Gather the children in a circle around the wall so that all can see.

Say: **Let's pretend that this is part of a big wall that surrounded the city where God's people lived. The wall kept them safe from wild animals and the bad people that tried to hurt them. But a strong army knocked down the wall and stole all of the people's good things.** On your signal, let children tear down the wall.

Ask: • **How would you feel if your house had a gate and someone smashed it and came in?**

Say: **All the people were sad when the wall was broken, and no one wanted to fix it. After many years, they forgot about their broken wall, but God didn't. God loved them and wanted them to feel his protection from the city wall again.**

God knew just whom he could use to get everyone excited about repairing and building up the

walls around the city. There was one man who loved God, and his name was Nehemiah. Nehemiah told all of the people that God would help them fix their wall. At first, the people were too sad to want to fix their wall. Nehemiah helped them see that God would help them.** Instruct the children to start rebuilding their wall. Then continue the Bible story.

As the people worked, some mean people who didn't want the wall to be fixed began to make fun of them. They said that God's people weren't strong enough to finish the wall. They might have said things like "Ha-ha! You can't do it."

Ask: • **How do you feel when someone calls you names or makes fun of you?**

• **How do you think God's people felt when they were being made fun of?**

Say: **They got discouraged and wanted to stop working. But Nehemiah reminded them that God would help them and that God makes them strong.** Have the children make strong muscles. **The people worked hard and finished building the walls of the city.** Have the children finish building the wall. When they have finished, lead them in shouting, "Hip, hip, hurray! God can use us!"

Can't find building blocks on short notice? Roll up old newspapers into logs. Use masking tape to keep the "logs" from unrolling, and let the children crisscross and stack them like pillars.

Esther Saves God's People

CD 12 track 2

Esther's Song

Sing "Esther's Song" to the tune of "Ten Little Indians."

When Mordecai told me the news (*point to yourself*)
That Haman planned to kill the Jews,
I knew right then that I (*place one palm up*)
must choose (*place the other palm up*)
To do a scary thing! (*Place both hands on cheeks, and show a scared expression.*)

I bowed before King Xerxes' feet (*bow down low*)
And asked if he would come and eat (*continue to bow and place both hands out*)

A feast with Haman and with me,
And the king said he would come. (*Stand up straight, looking pleased.*)

I told the king of Haman's plan (*point and shake index finger*)
To kill the Jews in all the land.
Guards took away the wicked man. (*Place hands behind back as if handcuffed.*)
And my people were saved that day! (*Turn around, shaking hands on each side of body.*)

Brave Esther

You can use this finger play to teach children the story of Esther. Little ones can learn that they can turn to God in prayer when they are afraid, just as Esther did.

Sometimes we are afraid and don't know what to do (*shrug shoulders*),

Like when the big dog barks, "Ruff! Ruff!" (*make barking sounds*)
Or when the thunder crashes. (*Clap hands together loudly.*)

When it's dark (*cover eyes with hands*)

Or, oh, so cold (*shiver as if cold*)

Or we break something and have to tell mom (*look surprised*),

Should we hide? (*Cover eyes.*)

Oh, no! Oh, no! (*Wag finger.*)

When Esther was afraid, she prayed. (*Make praying hands.*)

God helped her to be brave. (*Make strong arms.*)

So when the big dog barks, "Ruff! Ruff!" (*make barking sounds*)
Or when the thunder crashes. (*Clap hands together loudly.*)

When it's dark *(place hands over eyes)*

Or, oh, so cold *(shiver as if cold)*

Or we break something and have to tell mom
(look surprised),

Should we hide? *(Cover eyes with hands.)*

Oh, no! Oh, no! *(Wag finger.)*

We can pray like Esther 'cause God will show us what to do. *(Make praying hands.)*

Esther Saves God's People

Esther (various verses)

Bible Point: God will help us be brave.

Esther became aware of an evil plot to hurt God's people. As you share the story of Esther, you'll teach children that God helps them do the right thing, even when it might be scary.

Bring a large stack of paper (preferably taken from a recycle bin) for this activity.

Gather the children. Open your Bible to the book of Esther, and show the children the words.

Say: **We're going to hear a story about a woman to whom God gave courage. Each time we hear about someone showing courage, roll up a few pieces of paper and put them under your shirt like muscles. Our muscles will remind us that God gives us courage.**

Today's lesson comes from the book of Esther. One day Queen Esther learned that a bad man named Haman wanted to hurt all of God's people. Have the children cry, "Help us, God!" **Queen Esther knew she had to tell the king, but she was afraid. In those days, if you went to see the king without being invited, the king might hurt you if he didn't like it.** Have the children cry, "Help us, God!" **Esther needed to be brave** (have the children show strong arms), **but she was so afraid.**

Ask: • **Have you ever been afraid?**

• **What do you do when you are afraid?**

Say: **Esther prayed to God for three days** (have the children make praying hands), **asking God to help her be brave.** Have the children put a few paper wads

under their shirts and show strong arms and chests. **She visited the king's palace and invited the king and evil Haman to her house for dinner.** Have the children put more paper wads under their shirts.

The king was happy to come for dinner.

Ask: • **Have you ever acted brave, even when you were scared inside? What happened?**

Say: **The king and Haman came for dinner, and Esther invited them back for a special meal. During that meal, Esther told the king about Haman's evil plan to hurt God's people.** (Have the children cry, "Help us, God!") **The king had *Haman* hurt instead. The king passed a special law to protect God's people.** Have children shout, "Yeah!" and flex their muscles.

Ask: • **What did Esther do that helped her be brave?**

• **What will help us be brave?**

Say: **Our courage and strength doesn't come from our muscles; it comes from God. God can help us be brave.**

Job Is Faithful

Did You Hear About God's Servant?

cd2 track 3

Sing "Did You Hear About God's Servant?" to the tune of "Did You Ever See a Lassie?"

Did you hear about God's servant (*cup hand behind ear*),
God's servant, God's servant?
Did you hear about God's servant (*cup hand behind opposite ear*),
[Clap, clap] **God's servant named Job?** (*Put hands on hips.*)

He loved God. (*Cross arms on chest.*)
He served God. (*Pretend to dig with a shovel.*)
Even when it was hard! (*Pretend to lift a really heavy rock.*)

Did you hear about God's servant (*cup hand behind ear*),
God's servant named Job?

Hanging Tough

You can use this finger play to give your children an example of what it means to be a faithful friend to God, even when times get tough.

Job loved God (*hug yourself*)

And always took time to pray. (*Make praying hands.*)

Satan thought if Job's life got tough (*hold fists in front of you*),

Job's love would go away. (*Wave goodbye.*)

Satan took away Job's cattle (*push arms away and say, "Moo"*)

And his sheep and house, too. (*Push arms away and say, "Baa."*)
But Job loved God and kept his faith (*fold hands in prayer*),
And so can you! (*Point to each other.*)

Job Stays Faithful in Hard Times

Job 1:1–2:10; 42:1-6, 10-17

Bible Point: Keep loving God, even on bad days.

The details of Satan's challenge to God are hard for many adults to reconcile, let alone for preschoolers. But preschoolers can understand that they can be like Job and continue to love God, even when bad things happen.

Before class, cut out two heart shapes from red or pink construction paper for each child. Give each child one paper heart.

Say: **Satan is a bad angel who tries to trick people to stop being friends with God. One day Satan decided that he would trick Job into being mad at God by hurting Job. Maybe Job would be so mad and sad that he would decide that God wasn't good anymore. Let's help Job stay true to God by shouting, "Keep loving God!" to Job at different times throughout the Bible story.** Practice a few times with children.

First Satan tried to hurt Job by sending bad men to come and hurt his oxen and donkeys and servants that took care of these animals. Have each child tear off a piece of his or her paper heart and set the piece on the floor in front of him or her. **Job was sad, but he kept loving God.** Have kids shout, "Keep loving God!"

Next Satan tried to hurt Job by sending a fire from the sky that hurt Job's sheep and his servants. Have each child tear off a piece of his or her paper heart and set the piece on the floor in front of him or her. **Job was sad, but he kept loving God.** Have kids shout, "Keep loving God!"

Next Satan hurt Job by sending mean men to hurt all of Job's camels and servants. Have each child tear off a piece of his or her paper heart and set the piece on the floor in front of him or her. **Job was sad, but he kept loving God.** Have kids shout, "Keep loving God!"

Then Satan saw that he couldn't trick Job into hating God, so he knocked down a house where all of Job's children were eating. All of Job's children died. Have each child tear off a piece of his or her paper heart and set the piece on the floor in front of him or her. **Job was sad, but he kept loving God.** Have kids shout, "Keep loving God!"

Satan tried one last time to trick Job into hating God. He gave Job painful sores and bumps all over his body. Have each child tear off a piece of his or her paper heart and set the piece on the floor in front of him or her. **Job was sad, but he kept loving God.** Have kids shout, "Keep loving God!"

Even though Satan took away everything Job had and made Job sick, Job kept loving God. God saw that Job kept loving him, even when it was hard.

God made Job feel better. Give each child a second heart. **God gave him gold, cattle, and, best of all, ten wonderful children for Job to love. We can choose to keep loving God too. We can love God when it is easy and when it is hard.**

Ask: • **When do you love God?**
• **Why do you love God?**

Say: **We can keep loving God when we have good days and when we have bad days because God is always with us, loving us.**

The Lord Is My Shepherd

The Lord Is My Shepherd •

cd2 track 4

Sing "The Lord Is My Shepherd" to the tune of "The Mulberry Bush."

The Lord is my shepherd (*point up*),
My shepherd, my shepherd. (*Pretend to hold and pet a lamb.*)
The Lord is my shepherd (*point up*),
I shall not want. (*Shake head "no."*)

The Lord is my shepherd (*point up*),
My shepherd, my shepherd. (*Pretend to hold and pet a lamb.*)
The Lord is my shepherd (*point up*),
I shall not want. (*Shake head "no."*)

God Is Our Shepherd •

God takes care of us, just as a good shepherd takes care of his sheep. Teach children that God takes care of everyone and he loves us all. Throughout this finger play, use the index finger of one hand to point to each finger in order, beginning with the thumb, to name the "mom," "dad," "boy," "girl," and "baby."

Five little sheep in the Lord's care. (*Hold up five fingers.*)

A mom and a dad, a boy and a girl, and a baby over there. (*Point to each finger on hand.*)

God is the shepherd, and we are all his sheep. (*Hold up one finger, then continue wiggling fingers on opposite hand.*)

A mom and a dad, a boy and a girl, and a baby for God to keep. (*Point to each finger on hand.*)

God gives us rest and shows us the way. (*Rest head on hands.*)

A mom and a dad, a boy and a girl, and baby— hurray! (*Point to each finger on hand.*)

God keeps us safe and comforts me. (*Hug yourself.*)

A mom and dad, a boy and girl, and baby; you see? (*Point to each finger on hand.*)

God gives us good food and a cup that over- flows. (*Pretend to eat.*)

For mom and dad, boy and girl, and baby, God's love shows! (*Point to each finger on hand.*)

We'll live in God's house through the forgive- ness of his love. (*Hold arms out like a cross.*)

Mom and dad, boy and girl, and baby—we'll live with God above! (*Point to each finger on hand.*)

The Lord Is My Shepherd

Psalm 23

Bible Points: God will take care of us.

David sings of his trust in the Lord in Psalm 23. As you teach this lesson, remember that you are showing your children that God will take care of their every need.

Before you begin, gather the following supplies: a sheet of white bulletin board paper about five feet long to make a mural, cotton balls, construction paper in a variety of colors, markers, pretzel sticks, baby oil, and white glue. Attach the bulletin board paper to a blank wall at your children's eye level. Place the other supplies on a nearby table.

Read the paraphrased lines of the psalm, as children create murals.

Say: **The Lord is my shepherd. A shepherd's job is to take care of his sheep. God is our shepherd, and we are his sheep. God will take care of us, just like a shepherd takes care of his sheep.** Starting on the left side of the bulletin board paper, have each child glue one cotton ball "sheep" onto the paper. As the children are gluing their cotton balls onto the paper, draw a large stick-figure shepherd above the cotton balls.

Sheep love to rest in soft, green grass, near cool waters. A shepherd makes sure that his sheep have a place to rest. God gives us homes for us to rest in. Have the children tear strips of green construction paper and glue them around the sheep. Draw a large circle next to the sheep, and have the children tear strips of blue construction paper to glue inside for the water area.

God leads us on the right path. God shows us right from wrong. Let your children use a brown marker to draw line-type paths in the next section of the mural.

God takes care of us, even when we're afraid. A shepherd uses a long stick called his staff to make the sheep obey and to protect the sheep from wild animals that might want to hurt them. God takes care of us. Have each child glue one pretzel-stick "staff" onto the paper, next to the paths.

God takes care of our needs. He gives us good food to eat. Have the children draw squares to represent tables. If time permits, have your children glue precut magazine pictures of food onto the tables.

We are very special to God. In Bible days, people poured oil onto the heads of some of their guests to show how special they were. Give each child a cotton ball that has been dipped in baby oil. Show the children how to dab the cotton balls onto the paper to leave oily spots.

Not only does God take care of the things we need—such as food, water, families, and houses—but he gives us extra things, too. "Our cup runs over"—that's a saying that means we have lots and lots of good things. Quickly sketch a very large cup. Have the children tear and glue brown construction paper strips inside the cup.

God wants us to live with him forever. We live with him now by having him in our hearts. And we can live with him forever in heaven by trusting Jesus as our Savior to take care of us. Draw the outline of a large house. Have children draw themselves inside the house.

Ask: • **What are some ways God takes care of you and your family?**

Say: **Always remember that God will take care of you.**

Isaiah Is Sent

God Is Holy

cd2 track 5

Have your children stand and sing "God Is Holy" to the tune of "London Bridge." Try having the children walk in a circle as they do the motions.

I will sing and shout his praise (*place hands around mouth*),
Shout his praise, shout his praise.
I will sing and shout his praise
'cause God is holy.

God is holy; yes, he is. (*Point up.*)
Yes, he is. Yes, he is.

God is holy; yes, he is.
And I will praise him.

I will sing and shout his praise (*place hands around mouth*),
Shout his praise, shout his praise.
I will sing and shout his praise
'cause God is holy.

God Is in the Temple

The children will enjoy doing this action finger play while they learn about their awesome, holy God.

God is in the Temple. (*Touch fingertips over head.*)

Isaiah saw him there.
God's robe was long and flowing. (*Bring hands down to the floor.*)

There were angels in the air! (*Spread arms out like a bird.*)

The angels sang and praised (*cup hands to mouth*)

With smiles on their faces. (*Smile.*)
Their praises shook the Temple (*shake body*),

And smoke filled all the places. (*Wave hands in air.*)

One angel touched Isaiah. (*Touch mouth.*)

"Who will share my decree?" (*Shrug shoulders.*)

Isaiah said, "I will go! (*Hold arms up to God.*)

Here I am! Send me!" (*Point to yourself.*)

Isaiah Is Sent

Isaiah 6:1-8

Bible Point: God is holy.

Just before Isaiah is commissioned, he sees the splendor and holiness of the Lord. As you tell this story to your children, remember that you are telling them of God's holiness.

Before you begin, lay a blanket or two down on the floor, and then invite your children to sit on it with you.

Say: **Isaiah was a man who loved and obeyed God. God wanted to use Isaiah to tell his people to stop doing bad things and to do what was right. Isaiah saw God's glory.**

Ask: • **Do you know what glory is?**

Say: **Glory is God's goodness, power, and beauty. God is so powerful, good, and beautiful that he is brighter than the sun! Isaiah saw that God is holy.**

Ask: • **What does it mean to be holy?**

Say: **God is holy because he has never sinned. He has never done anything that is wrong—ever. God is perfect and holy.**

Each time children hear the words "God is holy," have them shout, "Holy, holy, holy!" like the angels.

Say: **Isaiah said, "I saw the Lord, seated on a throne, high and lifted up." God is holy.** Have children say, "Holy, holy, holy!" **God was sitting on a huge, fancy chair called a throne. God is so big. God's throne must be enormous! God is holy.** Have children say, "Holy, holy, holy!"

Ask: • **What colors do you think were on God's throne?**

Say: **Isaiah said that the robe God was wearing filled the whole room in which God sat. The Bible says that God's robe was big and wonderful! God's robe would fill the entire room we're in and every other room in this building! God is holy.** Have children say, "Holy, holy, holy!"

Ask: • **How many rooms do you think God's robe would fill?**

Say: **Then Isaiah saw angels with wings. They were called "seraphs," and they sang,** **"Holy, holy, holy is the Lord." God is holy.** Have children say, "Holy, holy, holy!" **The angels praised God so loudly and beautifully that it made the doors of the Temple shake, and the Temple was filled with smoke.**

Ask: • **How would you feel if you heard angels singing praises to God?**

Say: **God is holy!** Have children say, "Holy, holy, holy!"

Then one of the angels touched Isaiah's mouth and said to Isaiah, "Your sins are forgiven." Only God can forgive sins! Only God is holy! Have children say, "Holy, holy, holy!"

Then Isaiah heard God ask, "Whom will I send?"

Ask: • **What do you think Isaiah said?**

• **What would you say to God?**

Say: **Isaiah answered God and said, "Send me, God, send me." Isaiah told God that he would do God's job. Isaiah saw how awesome and holy God is. God is holy!** Have children say, "Holy, holy, holy!"

Daniel Is Safe in the Lions' Den

Daniel's Rap

Have the children stand and do the motions while they say "Daniel's Rap."

1. God wants you to pray to him,
And he won't care, no matter when.
Day or night, he's there for you.
He hears your prayers and answers, too!

(Chorus)
I don't care what the people say *(cup hands around mouth)*;
I'm gonna pray to God anyway! *(Drop to knees.)*
Claws 'n' laws won't keep me away *(make clawing motion)*;
I'm gonna pray to God anyway! *(Drop to knees.)*

2. Just like Daniel in the den,
God hears prayers, no matter when!

If trouble's got the best of you,
There's just one thing for you to do!
(Chorus.)

3. King Darius, he made a law;
To break it meant the lion's jaw.
But even though fear made him hop,
Daniel said, "I'll *never* stop!" 'cause…
(Chorus.)

4. So if worries and fears are bringin' you down,
And it feels like lions are chasin' you 'round,
Well, just stop and start to pray,
And God may send an angel your way!

Finger Food

Here is a fun finger play that the children will enjoy doing over and over. The repetition will also help your children gain mastery over the Bible story.

Hungry, hungry lions, do not roar! *(Wag finger.)*

Hungry, hungry lions, lie down on the floor.
(Lay head on hands.)

Hungry, hungry lions, the angel shut your mouth. *(Place both hands over mouth.)*

Hungry, hungry lions, God let Daniel out.
(Point away.)

Daniel Is Safe in the Lions' Den

Daniel 6:1-23

Bible Point: God is with us when we pray.

Daniel's insistence on maintaining his relationship with God through prayer caused him to be placed in a pit full of hungry lions. God honored Daniel's prayers and prevented the lions from hurting him. As you teach your children about the importance of prayer and God's friendship, remember that you are also developing awareness in your children that God is with them when they pray, just as he was with Daniel.

Before you begin, use masking tape to make a circle on the floor, large enough for the children to be able to move around inside. Have your children begin sitting around the outside of the circle. Give each child a paper plate folded in half to be the mouth of the lion. Enthusiastically read the Bible story and act out the motions. Your children will probably want to repeat the Bible story again.

Say: **Daniel loved God. He prayed every day.** (*Make praying hands.*)

But bad men didn't like him. They wished he would go away. (*Wag finger, then point away.*)

They made a bad law that said, "Pray only to the king." (*Make a triangle with fingers, then place them on head.*)

Daniel prayed to God; he did not change a thing. (*Make praying hands.*)

They threw him in the lion house (*stand up and jump inside the circle*)

Where the lions would make him lunch. (*Pretend to be a lion and crawl, holding paper plate in mouth.*)

Daniel prayed that the lions wouldn't munch. (*Open and close the paper-plate mouth.*)

Daniel prayed to God; he did not change a thing. (*Kneel and pretend to pray.*)

God sent an angel to handle everything. (*Stand up and "fly" around inside the circle.*)

"Close your mouths, lions. You may not have a bite. (*Clap hands closed.*)

God is saving Daniel. No food for you tonight." (*Wag finger, then jump out of the circle.*)

Ask: • **When do you pray to God?**

• **What happened when Daniel prayed to God?**

Say: **God is with us when we pray, just as he was with Daniel.**

Tip From the Trenches

If you have a large class, make a tape circle for every ten children.

Jonah Learns to Obey God

Why Jonah Obeys

cd2 track 7

Sing "Why Jonah Obeys" to the tune of "Take Me Out to the Ball Game."

Jonah didn't obey God. *(Wag finger.)*

Jonah told God, "No!" *(Place hand in front to show "stop.")*

He did what he wanted.

He wouldn't obey *(wag finger)*

'Til a big fish came and took him away. *(Place arms in front and close them like a big mouth.)*

Jonah, he always listens. *(Place hand behind ear and lean.)*

He obeys God's every wish. *(Point up.)*

He spent one! two! three! nights and days *(hold up appropriate fingers)*

In the belly of a fish. *(Pat tummy.)*

We Must Obey the Lord

We sometimes find it difficult to obey God. God's ways are always best; the sooner we learn to obey immediately, the happier we will be!

God said to Jonah, "Walk to Ninevah." *(Walk fingers up arm.)*

God said to Jonah, "Their evil, it must stop!" *(Hold hand up, palm out.)*

Tell the people there they must obey the Lord. *(Cup hands around mouth.)*

Tell the people there to stop and obey the Lord. *(Hold hand up, palm out.)*

Jonah had other plans. He didn't obey the Lord. *(Wag finger.)*

Jonah had other plans. He jumped on a ship. "All aboard?" *(Cup one hand, then "jump" index and middle fingers of opposite hand into palm.)*

The boat rocked and tossed about 'cause God sent a storm to them. *(Move cupped hand with fingers inside back and forth.)*

The boat rocked and tossed about 'cause Jonah didn't obey again! *(Wag finger.)*

When Jonah got tossed overboard, a fish quickly gobbled him up. *(Dramatically open and close mouth.)*

When Jonah got tossed overboard, he saw the fish close up.

After three days the fish spit Jonah upon the dry, green land. *(Spread hands out with palms down.)*

After three days the fish spit Jonah, just as God had planned. *(Show thumbs up.)*

Jonah told the people to change and stop their wicked ways. *(Hold hand up, palm out.)*

Jonah told the people to change, and they began to praise. *(Clap hands and look up.)*

So Ninevah turned away from evil and all their sin.

So Ninevah followed God with a great big grin!

Jonah Learns to Obey God

Jonah

Bible Point: Obey God.

Jonah learned the hard way that we must obey God or suffer the consequences. Help your children see how important it is to obey the first time they're asked, by emphasizing good consequences that may follow their obedience.

Before you begin, gather a large sheet and masking tape. Drape the sheet over a table, leaving one end open for the fish's mouth. Put masking tape on the floor in the shape of a boat large enough for the whole class to sit inside.

Have the children stand on the outside of the boat shape to begin the Bible story.

Say: **God told Jonah to go to Ninevah and preach there. He wanted Jonah to tell them to stop doing wrong things and to do what was right. But Jonah didn't want to go there. He didn't want to obey God. Jonah thought he could hide from God, so he jumped aboard a ship that would sail in the opposite direction.**

Have the children join you inside the outline of the boat.

Say: **Let's make the sounds of the ocean with our hands.** Show your children how to slide their palms back and forth to make a swishing sound. Have them softly say, "Swish, swish," each time they swish their hands.

Jonah's boat sailed across the water. Continue making the sounds of the water with your hands. **Let's rock back and forth, just as Jonah's ship is rocking.** Have children make the swishing noises; say, "Swish, swish"; and rock back and forth for about ten seconds.

Soon a terrible storm came up. Let's make the thunder sound. Have children clap their hands loudly. **Now let's make the ocean sounds, louder and faster.** Have the children swish their hands faster. **Now let's rock even harder.** Have the children sway back and forth faster.

The men on the ship wondered what to do. When they found out that Jonah had caused God to be angry for disobeying, they tossed him in the water.** Have kids pretend to toss something far away. **And a giant fish swallowed him.** Point out the sheet-covered table, and tell them to pretend it's the giant fish.

While Jonah was in the fish's belly, he asked God to forgive him and promised to obey. Let's take turns being Jonah in the fish's belly. Let children take turns going inside the "giant fish." As they enter, have each of the children say, "I must obey God."

When Jonah promised to obey, God let the fish spit Jonah out onto the sand. Then Jonah went to Ninevah and told the people to turn from their evil ways and make good choices. The people obeyed, and God saved Ninevah from being destroyed.

Ask: • **When have you obeyed? What happened?**

Say: **Jonah finally obeyed God. We can obey God too.**

Tip From the Trenches

Leave the "fish's mouth" open so that children will not be afraid when they go inside.

People Get Ready for Jesus

Are You Ready?

cd2 track 8

Give all the children musical instruments, a few bells strung on a piece of yarn, or simple craft sticks to hit together. Have the children stand up or walk in a circle playing their instruments while they sing "Are You Ready?" to the tune of "The Battle Hymn of the Republic."

Christmastime is coming;
It's a special time of year.
We must all get ready;
Jesus' birth is almost here.
We must open up our hearts
For the baby, oh, so dear.
Are you ready for our heavenly king?

Everybody's getting ready.
Everybody's getting ready.
Everybody's getting ready,
Ready for our heavenly king.

A Place for Baby Jesus

Children see adults prepare for Christmas by decorating, buying gifts, and trimming the tree. Use this finger play to help them understand that they can get ready for Jesus' coming by making their hearts clean for him. The children will act out cleaning up a nursery room for Jesus.

Baby Jesus is coming! Is everything in place?
(Draw heart shape on chest.)

We will put away our fighting. *(Pretend to pick up something and put it away.)*

We will put away our lying. *(Repeat motion.)*
We will put away our stealing. *(Repeat motion.)*
These aren't things that baby Jesus would like.
(Pretend to rock baby in arms.)

We will paint our room with kindness. *(Pretend to paint the air.)*

We will give him gifts of love. *(Hug yourself.)*

We will be ready for baby Jesus. *(Pretend to rock baby in arms.)*

We will welcome him with love. *(Hug yourself.)*

People Get Ready for Jesus

Isaiah 9:6; Jeremiah 33:14-16; Luke 3:7-18

Bible Point: We should get ready for Jesus.

The Christmas season is filled with joyful preparations—cleaning, shopping, and baking. John the Baptist told his people how to prepare for the coming of the Messiah by turning away from sinful behavior. As you teach your children about John the Baptist's ministry, you can help them understand that they can prepare a clean heart for Jesus this Christmas season.

Before you begin, have pieces of newspaper or scraps of paper ready. Each child will need one piece. Invite the children to join you in sitting in a circle on the floor. Open your Bible to Luke, and show children the words.

Say: **Today's Bible story comes from the book of Luke in the Bible. John the Baptist told the people to get ready for Jesus to come because he would be a special king that would come to help people. John the Baptist saw that people weren't ready for Jesus, so God used him to help show the people how to get ready for Jesus.**

Some people were stealing. Give each child a piece of newspaper. Tell children to wad up the newspapers and put them behind their backs. Then direct the children to take the wads that are behind the backs of the children sitting next to them. **And they took things that didn't belong to them.**

Some people would not share with each other. Have each child turn to a partner next to him or her, grab hands, and gently rock back and forth as if playing Tug of War. **And they struggled back and forth.**

Some people were telling mean lies about other people. Have children pretend to whisper into the ears of the children sitting next to them. **And they were not telling the truth.**

Some people were being bullies and picking on weaker people. Have the children put their hands on their hips, look at each of their friends sitting next to them, and say, "Na, na, na, na, na!" **And they were not being very nice.**

John the Baptist told the people that they needed to clean up their messes. They needed to clean up their hearts. They needed to tell God they were sorry so they could make a brand-new start.

Let's get ready for Jesus. Let's clean up our hearts. Let's be kind and friendly so we can make a brand-new start.

John the Baptist told the people who were stealing to stop. Have kids give back the wads of paper.

He told the people who were being selfish to share. Have kids give their wads to the people sitting next to them.

He told the people who were lying to tell the truth. Have kids shake hands with the children on both sides of them.

He told the people who were being bullies to stop. Have kids give high fives.

John the Baptist told the people that they needed to clean up their messes. They needed to clean up their hearts. They needed to tell God they were sorry so they could make a brand-new start.

Let's get ready for Jesus. Let's clean up our hearts. Let's be kind and friendly so we can make a brand-new start.

Ask: • **What are some kind actions that you like people to do for you?**

Say: **We can get our hearts ready for Jesus this Christmas by doing things that make him happy. If we catch ourselves doing things that make our lives dirty, we can stop, tell God we are sorry, and then start doing things that please God and make him and others happy.**

Jesus Is Born

Jesus Came •

cd2 track 9

Give the children bells to shake while they sing "Jesus Came" to the tune of "Jingle Bells."

Jesus came.
Jesus came.
Jesus came to show
That he's God's Son and he's the one
God promised long ago.

Jesus came.
Jesus came.
Jesus came to show
That he's God's Son and he's the one
God promised long ago.

Excited About Jesus •

This finger play can help children catch the excitement that surrounded Jesus' birth. The repeating phrase, "Glory to the Lord," will create a rhythm that will make the finger play memorable and emphasize how special Jesus' birth was. Tell your children that you will point to them when it's their turn to say, "Glory to the Lord." Practice a few times and then begin.

The Angel visited Mary.
Glory to the Lord! *(Have kids shout the words and shake hands above heads.)*

"God will give you baby Jesus." *(Pretend to cradle and rock a baby)*

Glory to the Lord! *(Have kids shout the words and shake hands above heads.)*

Mary said "yes" to God.
Glory to the Lord! *(Have kids shout the words and shake hands above heads.)*

God gave her baby Jesus. *(Pretend to cradle and rock a baby.)*

Glory to the Lord! *(Have kids shout the words and shake hands above heads.)*

Angels visited the shepherds.
Glory to the Lord! *(Have kids shout the words and shake hands above heads.)*

And told them Jesus came. *(Pretend to cradle and rock a baby.)*

Glory to the Lord! *(Have kids shout the words and shake hands above heads.)*

To love and set them free. *(Hug yourself.)*

Glory to the Lord! *(Have kids shout the words and shake hands above heads.)*

The shepherds ran to Jesus. *(Run two fingers up arm.)*

Glory to the Lord! *(Have kids shout the words and shake hands above heads.)*

They worshipped the baby King.
Glory to the Lord! *(Have kids shout the words and shake hands above heads.)*

They told everyone they could.
Glory to the Lord! *(Have kids shout the words and shake hands above heads.)*

Jesus Is Born

Luke 1:26-45; 2:1-20

Bible Point: We can celebrate Jesus' birth.

By leading the children enthusiastically, you'll help them discover the joy of Jesus' birth.

Gather the children in a circle, and let your children open your Bible to the book of Luke. Pass your Bible around the circle so your children can touch and see the words.

Say: **Today's Bible story comes from the book of Luke. There are many angels in this story. An angel is a special messenger from God. Every time you hear me say, "Angel," shout, "Praise to God!"**

One day an angel (have children shout, "Praise to God!") **visited a woman named Mary. The angel** (have children shout, "Praise to God!") **told Mary that God would give her a special baby named Jesus. Jesus would be God's very own Son, but Mary was afraid. Can you pretend to be afraid?** Have children show what they feel like when they're afraid. **But Mary trusted God.**

Mary and her husband, Joseph, had to go on a long trip back to the town where Joseph was born.

When it was time for God to give baby Jesus to Mary and Joseph, they had to find a place to stay for the night. But no one had room.

The only place for Mary to rest was in a stable where farm animals lived—in a barn.

Ask: • **Can you name an animal that lives in a barn?**

• **What sound does that animal make?**

Say: **These are some of the animals and sounds that might have filled the place where Jesus was born. Mary wrapped baby Jesus in cloth to keep him warm and laid him in a manger to sleep.** Have the children pretend to wrap a blanket around a baby and rock it back and forth.

Meanwhile, shepherds were taking care of their sheep in the fields. Have children make sheep sounds. **It was late at night when angels** (have children shout, "Praise to God!") **appeared to the shepherds. The whole sky was filled with angels.** (Have children shout, "Praise to God!") **They told the shepherds that baby Jesus was born and that he would take away the bad things people did. The angels** (Have children shout, "Praise to God!") **told the shepherds that they could find baby Jesus in the city of Bethlehem. So the shepherds ran to find Jesus—the baby King that God had promised to send for so many years.**

When the shepherds saw baby Jesus, they were so happy! They told everyone what the angels had said. Have children shout, "Praise to God!" **"Jesus came to take away our sins,"** they said. **The shepherds were so happy that God gave us baby Jesus!**

Ask: • **How do people act when a baby is born?**

• **How do you act when you're happy about something and want to celebrate it?**

Say: **We can tell others about Jesus and celebrate that Jesus was born to take away all the bad things we do.**

Wise Men Worship Jesus

This Is the Way the Wise Men Came

cd2 track 10

Sing "This Is the Way the Wise Men Came" to the tune of "The Mulberry Bush."

This is the way the wise men came *(bounce up and down as if riding a camel),*
Wise men came, wise men came.
This is the way the wise men came
To visit baby Jesus. *(Make cradling motions with arms.)*

This is the way the star shone bright *(raise arms above head and open and close fingers),*
Star shone bright, star shone bright.
This is the way the star shone bright
Over baby Jesus. *(Make cradling motion with arms.)*

Baby Shower

Have your children sit down with you for this finger play.

Wise men saw a special star and knew a King was born. *(Make a circle with hands and place them on head.)*

They made special gifts and traveled very far. *(Shield eyes with one hand, and pretend to look far away.)*

The special star showed the way to find the baby King. *(Make a circle with hands and place them on head.)*

They gave him gifts; they bowed down low while baby Jesus lay. *(Make a circle with hands and place them on head.)*

What will we give to our King born on Christmas Day? *(Pretend to rock baby in arms.)*

We give our love; we give our lives *(hug yourself);*

We give our everything. *(Stretch arms out on each side.)*

Wise Men Worship Jesus

Matthew 2:1-12

Bible Point: We can give gifts to Jesus.

Children love to give and receive gifts at Christmastime. As you teach this lesson to your preschoolers, you will help them see that they can give Jesus good gifts also.

Before you begin, mold a one-foot-long piece of aluminum foil into the shape of star.

Gather the class around you in a circle on the floor. Open your Bible to the book of Matthew, and pass the Bible around the circle for children to see the words.

Say: **Today's Bible adventure is from the book of Matthew. In a country far away from where Jesus was born, there lived some wise men. The wise men had been watching a special star in the sky.** Hold the foil star over your head. **The wise men knew that God put this star in the sky to tell them that Jesus, the promised King, was born. They knew that if they followed the star, it would lead them to where the promised King would be.**

But first they wanted to prepare special gifts to give to Jesus. Let's pretend to make gifts for Jesus by shaping these pieces of foil into whatever you want. Give each child a piece of aluminum foil. Instruct kids to mold their foil into the shapes of gifts that they would have liked to give Jesus.

The wise men prepared gifts of gold and nice-smelling perfumes and spices. Then they followed the star. Hold up the star over your head, and lead the children to the opposite side of the room—around tables, chairs, and toys. Have a doll sitting in your dramatic play area, and tell the children that you will pretend that it's little Jesus.

When they found Jesus, they gave him their gifts. Have children set their foil gifts on the ground in front of the doll. **They worshipped Jesus. They were so happy that God helped them meet Jesus, the promised King.**

Ask: • **What do you think you might say to Jesus?**

• **If you were a wise man, what kind of a gift would you give to Jesus?**

Say: **We may not be rich or extra-smart like the wise men, but we can give special gifts to Jesus too.**

Jesus Grows Up

I Love Jesus

Group your children in small circles of about two or three. As they sing "I Love Jesus" to the tune of "London Bridge," have them skip, dance, or walk in a circle.

Jesus did just what was right,
Every day,
Every night.
He was pleasing in God's sight.
I love Jesus!

I can try to do what's right,
Every day,
Every night.
I'll be pleasing in God's sight.
I love Jesus!

Jesus Grows Up

As you say this finger play with your children, remind them that Jesus grew up, just like they're doing.

Jesus grew up bit by bit. (*Curl up pointer finger, then straighten it.*)
He grew up strong. (*Make strong arms.*)
He grew wise (*tap finger on side of head*)
But one day gave his family a big surprise. (*Show a surprised expression.*)

His family took a very long trip. (*Touch fingertips together to make a roof.*)
After they left (*point to wrist*),

No one did know (*walk fingers up arm*)
Where Jesus went. "Where did he go?" (*Shrug shoulders.*)

Jesus was not worried; for three days he stayed. (*Hold up three fingers.*)
In God's house (*touch fingertips together to make a roof*)
He learned and prayed. (*Make praying hands.*)
"My Father," he said, "I must obey." (*Point up.*)

Jesus Grows Up

Luke 2:39-52

Bible Point: God wants us to know him.

The Bible says little about Jesus' childhood but does say he grew in divine wisdom and grace. Children enjoy learning that Jesus was a child, just like they are. As you teach this lesson, help them imagine what Jesus must have been like as a child and how they can be like Jesus.

Have the children sit in a circle around you. Open your Bible to Luke 2, and show the children the words.

Say: **Today's Bible story is from the book of Luke. It is the story about how Jesus grew up as a child. When Jesus was born, he was just a little baby. Can you act like a newborn baby?** Lead your children in pretending to be babies.

One day Jesus learned how to crawl. Show me how you think Jesus would have crawled. Let your children crawl around for a few moments.

Jesus grew and grew and grew. Lead the children in crouching down and gradually standing up.

The Bible says Jesus was a strong little boy.

Show me your big, strong muscles. Lead the children in showing their strong muscles.

The Bible says Jesus was filled with wisdom and God's power, too. He loved God very much because he was God's only Son.

When Jesus was an older boy, his family went to visit the Temple—God's special house. The Temple was kind of like our church building. Jesus' family traveled with lots of friends. Have the children stand, link arms with two other friends, walk around the room for a few moments, and then sit down in another area of the room.

When Jesus and his family got to the Temple, they ate a special meal and talked about how well God treated them. Have all the children sit in a circle, and then give each of them a couple of crackers.

Ask: • **What had God done that was good?**

Say: **When it was time to go, everyone left to go back home.** Have children link arms and then walk back to the original story area. **After three days of traveling, Jesus' family realized that they had forgotten Jesus! They were so worried.** Have the children stand up and run in place.

Jesus' family asked everyone they knew, and they finally found Jesus back in the Temple—God's special house. Jesus was reading God's Word, talking with teachers, and asking lots of questions in the Temple. Jesus told his family not to worry about him. He wasn't lost. He reminded them that he was in the house of his Father, God, because he was God's Son!

Ask: • **What are some things you know about God?**

• **What do you want to know about God or Jesus?**

Say: **When we come to church, we learn about God and Jesus. When we ask our parents about God, we learn more about him. God wants us to know him like Jesus knows him.**

John Baptizes Jesus

God Loved Us

Sing "God Loved Us" to the tune of "The Muffin Man."

Chorus:
God loved us so very much (*hug yourself on each "very much"*),
Very much, very much.
God loved us so very much
That he gave his only Son. (*Point up and then down.*)

Jesus asked John to baptize him (*wiggle fingers over head on each "baptize him"*),
Baptize him, baptize him.
Jesus asked John to baptize him,

And Jesus made God happy. (*Point to smiling mouth.*)
(*Repeat chorus.*)

God told Jesus, "I love you, Son" (*make the sign for "I love you" for each "I love you, Son"*),
"I love you, Son," "I love you, Son."
God told Jesus, "I love you, Son.
You make me so happy!" (*Clasp hands in front of chest.*)
(*Repeat chorus.*)

Proud Father

You can use this finger play to let children know that God enjoys them. God loves us no matter what, but when we obey him, we can feel not only God's love but also that he is proud of us.

Jesus at the river (*make waves with both hands from side to side*),

He knew just what to do.
He wanted to please God (*give two thumbs up*)

In all that he would do.
He dipped under the water (*start with hands vertical, then lay them to one side*)

In front of all to see,
It's God that makes us clean. (*Rub hands together.*)

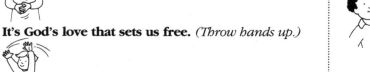

It's God's love that sets us free. (*Throw hands up.*)

God told Jesus that he loved him. (*Hug yourself.*)

God told Jesus he was proud. (*Give two thumbs up.*)

I betcha Jesus felt as happy as can be. (*Point to smile*)

Now Jesus *always* loves me. (*Hug yourself.*)

I know how to make him proud. (*Tap finger on side of head.*)

When I do my best to obey him (*point up*),

That's what makes him proud! (*Give two thumbs up.*)

John Baptizes Jesus

Mark 1:4-11

Bible Point: God was proud of Jesus.

During the account of Jesus' baptism, we are given a glimpse at the intimate relationship between God the Father and God the Son. The heavenly Father interrupts the baptism ceremony to interject an "I love you" and "I'm proud of you" to Jesus. As you teach this lesson to children, you can help them see how much their heavenly Father loves them.

Before you begin, get a large sheet or tablecloth. Ideally, you want to find something blue to represent the water, but in a pinch, the children's imagination can color the sheet blue.

Spread the sheet out on the floor. Then have the children sit in a circle around the sheet.

Say: **Our Bible story takes place at the Jordan River.** Have children hold onto the edge of the sheet and *gently* make waves up and down.

John the Baptist told many people about God. He told people to get ready for God's Son and to do things that make God happy. Any time someone said "yes" to wanting to make God happy, John would wash him or her in the river.

Have the children grab the sheet with both hands, stand up, and lift it over their heads. Let them make waves for a minute and then set the sheet back on the ground and sit down.

Say: **Jesus came to where John the Baptist was washing people. Jesus wanted everyone to know that he loved to make God happy, so he asked John to baptize him.**

Have the children grab the sheet with both hands, stand up, and lift it over their heads. Let them make waves for a minute and then set the sheet back on the ground and sit down.

Say: **Then God wanted to let Jesus know how happy Jesus made him. God talked and told everyone that Jesus was his Son and that Jesus made him very happy.**

Ask: • **How do you think Jesus felt hearing that he made God happy?**

• **How do you feel when your parents say nice things to you?**

Say: **God loves us, too, just because he made us.**

Ask: • **How does it feel knowing that God loves you?**

Say: **God is proud of us when we do things that make him happy.**

Ask: • **What can you do to make God proud?**

• **How does it feel knowing that God can be proud of you?**

For a large class, bring in two sheets so every child can participate.

Jesus Is Tempted

God Makes Me Strong

cd2 track 13

Sing "God Makes Me Strong" to the tune of "Down By the Bay."

God makes me strong (*flex arm muscles*)
So I can say (*point to mouth*),
"No, Satan, no! (*Shake head angrily.*)
You go away!" (*Point at the door.*)
God helps me do right (*lift up both hands, and look up toward God*)
So I can say (*point to mouth*),

"Following the rules (*tap face-up palm of one hand with index finger of other hand on the words* Following *and* rules)
Is always cool! (*Shout, "Cool!"*)
Just go away!" (*Shout these words with arms folded across chest.*)

You Can't Trick Me

Have your children sit in a circle and then stand up when they say the last line of the following rhyme.

You can't trick me, Satan. Go away. (*Wag finger.*)

This is what the Bible says. I must obey. (*Place hands together like a book, then show two thumbs up.*)

I can be like Jesus and say "No!" to what is wrong. (*Hold hand out with palm out.*)

I can say "No!" and stand up strong. (*Stand up and show strong arms.*)

Jesus Is Tempted

Luke 4:1-13

Bible Point: God can help us when we're tempted.

Preschoolers are still developing self-control and their ability to say "no" to things they know they should not do. By teaching this lesson, you are helping children begin to develop a strategy for dealing with temptation—stand up; say, "no"; and turn away.

Hold a bag of cookies or snacks and a bag of rocks or unwanted items behind your back. Without allowing children to see, put a snack in one hand and a rock in the other.

Allow each child to choose one of your hands. Open the hand the child chose. If the child chooses the undesirable item, allow him or her to have the snack.

Ask: • **How would you feel if you were given only the rock?**

Say: **In today's Bible story, Satan tried to trick Jesus into doing wrong things that would make God sad. Satan tried to get Jesus to make bad choices. During our Bible story, listen and be ready to stand up, turn around, and shout, "No! Go away!" each time you hear me say Satan's name.**

One day Jesus was in the desert and Satan (stand up, turn around, and shout, "No! Go away!") **came to try to trick Jesus into doing bad things. The first thing Satan** (stand up, turn around, and shout, "No! Go away!") **tried to do was have Jesus turn a rock into bread.** Show children a large rock. **That may sound like a silly temptation, but Jesus was really, really hungry because he hadn't eaten anything for a long, long time.**

Ask: • **Would you be tempted to make food for yourself if you were hungry?**

Say: **Jesus was probably tempted, but he didn't sin. He knew Satan** (stand up, turn around, and shout, "No! Go away!") **was actually asking Jesus to prove that he was God's Son and could do miracles. Jesus told Satan** (stand up, turn around, and shout, "No! Go away!") **that he didn't have to prove that he was God's Son—he already knew that. Yes, Jesus could have made the rock turn into bread, but that wasn't what the Bible said he should do. God helped Jesus when he was tempted, and God will help us.**

Another time Satan (stand up, turn around, and shout, "No! Go away!") **took Jesus to the top of the highest mountain where they could see the whole city in all its beauty and riches. He told Jesus to bow down to him and he would give Jesus all the power and riches in the world. But Jesus knew who created all the power and riches in the world. He knew who the Bible said is the only person to whom he should bow down.**

Ask: • **Who do you think created all the power and riches in the world?**

Say: **Jesus told Satan** (stand up, turn around, and shout, "No! Go away!") **that he didn't need power or riches. He knew that the Bible said God would give him all that he needed. Yes, Jesus could have bowed down, but that wasn't what the Bible said he should do. God helped Jesus when he was tempted, and God will help us.**

Satan (stand up, turn around, and shout, "No! Go away!") **tried to trick Jesus one last time. He told him to jump off the edge of a really high temple to prove that God loved him. Jesus knew what the Bible said. He knew God loved him. Jesus told Satan** (stand up, turn around, and shout, "No! Go away!") **that he didn't have to prove that God loved him—he already knew that. Yes, Jesus could have jumped off the temple and God would have saved him, but that wasn't what the Bible said he should do. Jesus told Satan** (stand up, turn around, and shout, "No! Go away!") **to go away and not to tempt the Lord God anymore.**

Satan (stand up, turn around, and shout, "No! Go away!") **finally went away because Jesus kept saying "no" to him and choosing what was right. We, too, can say "no" when we're tempted to do something that we know is wrong. God helped Jesus when he was tempted, and God will help us.**

Ask: • **When do you feel like you might make a wrong choice?**

• **Who can we ask to help us when we feel tempted to do wrong?**

• **How do you feel when you make a good choice?**

Say: **God is always there to help us when we feel tempted to do something wrong. All we have to do is remember to ask God for help, and he will help us. God helped Jesus when he was tempted, and God will help us.**

Jesus Turns Water Into Wine

Jesus Went to a Wedding

Sing "Jesus Went to a Wedding" to the tune of "Ninety-Nine Bottles of Pop."

When Jesus went to a wedding one day (*walk in a circle*),

His friends ran out of wine. (*Stop quickly and hold hands out to sides.*)

So Jesus made some.

He is God's Son.

He helped everything turn out fine. (*Reverse circle and march the other way for the second verse.*)

And Jesus knows when I'm hurting or sad.

He helps me know what to do.

He's the Son of God.

He's Jesus, the Lord.

I know that he cares for me, too!

Going to a Wedding!

When this finger play begins, it is modern day and you are preparing to attend a wedding. As you move through the play, today's story is reviewed and the children are once again reminded that Jesus is the one in whom to believe.

A bow in our hair; a tie 'round our neck. (*Pretend to straighten a tie.*)

Our faces are scrubbed; our teeth have been checked. (*Point to a big "toothy" smile.*)

We'll sit, oh, so quiet 'til the wedding is done (*place hands in lap*),

Then off to the party for lots of fun! (*Walk fingers up arm.*)

There'll be plenty of food; oh, please don't run out. (*Pretend to eat.*)

At the wedding in Cana, it made people pout. (*Show a sad face.*)

But Jesus was there to save the day! (*Two thumbs up.*)

His very first miracle made people say (*hold up one finger*),

"In him we believe, and we'll follow today." (*Walk two fingers on each hand away from you.*)

Jesus Turns Water Into Wine

John 2:1-11

Bible Point: We can believe in Jesus.

Weddings are exciting events, and the wedding in Cana was no exception. But at that wedding, the host ran out of drink. Mary turned to Jesus for help, telling the servants to do whatever Jesus said. After Jesus performed a miracle, the disciples knew they could believe in Jesus. As you teach this lesson, help your children realize they can believe in Jesus too.

Before you begin, you will need to have a package of pre-sweetened powdered drink mix for your children (check the serving sizes on the package). Pour the powdered drink mix into a dark pitcher, but *do not* add the water! Divide the appropriate amount of water for the drink mix between enough small paper cups for each child in your class to have one. Set the supplies, including a spoon, near your Bible story area.

Say: **Today we'll hear about a wedding that took place a long time ago. Let's look in our Bible in the book of John.** Open your Bible, and show the children the words. **If you have ever been a flower girl or a ring bearer in a wedding or have gone to a wedding, please stand up.** Have children sit back down if any of them are standing. **People go to weddings to help the bride and groom celebrate their exciting day. Many important and special people come to weddings— friends and relatives from everywhere.**

Jesus was at a wedding with his mother and some of his followers. Everyone was having a great time at the wedding party, until *it* happened. All of a sudden, they were out of drinks. The special wine that they were drinking was gone. Have children pretend to hold a glass upside down and look up inside.

Jesus' mother, Mary, told Jesus about it, then she told the servants to do whatever Jesus said to do. Jesus told the servants to take some empty water jars and fill them up with water. Let's fill up our pitcher with water. Have each child pour a cup

of water into the pitcher until the correct amount is added. Then give the water a little stir.

Next, Jesus told them to take a cup of water and give it to the man in charge of the wedding party. When the servants did this, the man in charge couldn't believe what he was tasting. It was the best drink they had at the entire party! It wasn't water anymore; Jesus had turned the water into a very yummy-tasting drink.

This was Jesus' very first miracle, and his followers saw that they could trust him. They believed in Jesus. We can believe in Jesus too! We can also trust Jesus. Let's taste our drink now and see how it tastes. Give each child a cup filled halfway with the drink they made.

Ask: • **What did Jesus do that caused people to believe in him?**

• **What do you believe about Jesus?**

Say: **Jesus wants us to believe in him. We can believe in Jesus.**

Tip From the Trenches

To really help the children feel like they're at a wedding, decorate the room to look like a wedding reception. Streamers, balloons, flowers, and a small cake could all help set the right mood!

Jesus Calls the Disciples

Disciples' Call

cd2 track 15

Invite your children to stand up and sing "Disciples' Call" to the tune of "My Bonnie Lies Over the Ocean."

Jesus saw Simon and Andrew
Tossing their nets to catch fish. *(Pretend to toss nets into the water.)*
Jesus saw Simon and Andrew *(shield eyes with hand, as if searching),*
And this was Jesus' wish:

Chorus:
"Come and follow. *(Motion to come along.)*
Oh, put down your nets. *(Bend down and touch the ground.)*
Come with me, with me! *(Motion to yourself.)*

Come and follow. *(Motion to come along.)*
Oh, put down your nets. *(Bend down and touch the ground.)*
Follow me!" *(Motion to yourself.)*

Jesus saw James and John
Fixing their nets to catch fish. *(Pretend to toss nets into the water.)*
Jesus saw James and John *(shield eyes with hand, as if searching),*
And this was Jesus' wish:
(Repeat chorus.)

Follow Me

Peter, Andrew, James, and John were just plain, ordinary men who left everything they had to follow Jesus. Never once do we get the idea that they hesitated or questioned their decision. As you do this finger play, remind the children that Jesus called and the disciples followed! He wants the same from each of us.

Simon, Andrew, and their great big nets were catching fish and getting wet. *(Shake as if all wet.)*

Jesus called to both of them, "Follow me, and we'll fish for men." *(Motion with hand to come.)*

James and John were in the boat, fixing their nets and staying afloat. *(Cup one hand and place two fingers of other hand inside.)*

Jesus called to both of them, "Follow me, and we'll fish for men." *(Motion with hand to come.)*

Two sets of brothers left all they had. They followed Jesus, and they were glad. *(Walk fingers on both hands, one in front of the other.)*

Jesus calls to me and you, "Follow me, and tell others, too!" *(Motion with hand to come.)*

Jesus Calls the Disciples

Mark 1:14-20

Bible Point: We can follow Jesus.

This Bible story is a wonderful reminder that Jesus values ordinary people and wants us to follow him—and he takes us just the way we are! As you tell today's Bible story, share with children that Jesus wants *all* of us to follow him and fish for men.

Before you begin, make a large outline of a boat on the floor with masking tape, and lay a blue sheet on the floor next to the boat to represent Lake Galilee.

Say: **Today our Bible story is found in the book of Mark.** Open your Bible, and show children the book of Mark. **This is a special story about two sets of brothers who were fishermen.**

Ask: • **When you go fishing at a lake or ocean, what do you catch?**

Say: **Simon and his brother, Andrew, were fishing on the shore of Lake Galilee, trying to catch fish for their families and to sell to others.** Encourage the children to stand alongside the blue sheet and pretend to fish.

One day Jesus came along and called out to them, "Simon and Andrew, come with me, and I will show you how to fish for men instead of for fish!"

"What? Fish for men? What is Jesus talking about?" they said. So the brothers followed Jesus. Have the children follow you and get inside the masking-tape boat.

As Jesus continued to walk along the shore of Galilee, he saw two more brothers. James and John were in their boat mending their nets. Encourage children to pretend they are repairing holes in their nets. **Jesus called out to them, too: "James, John, come with me, and I will show you how to fish for men instead of for fish!" James and John climbed out of their boat and followed Jesus.** Have the children get out of the

"boat," follow you over to the "sea," and sit down.

Ask: • **What do you think Jesus meant by "fishing for men"?**

Say: **Instead of catching fish, they were going to catch people. Now, they weren't really going to grab ahold of people and catch them, but they were going to go and tell as many people as they could about Jesus and his Father, God. Jesus wants each of us to follow him and fish for people who want to follow Jesus too.**

Let's sing and play a game that will help us understand. Let's go fishing for people! Help the children get into groups of four, and have two of the children form a bridge with their hands so the others can go under. Lead the children in singing "Come Follow Him" to the tune of "London Bridge."

Jesus says to come follow him,
Follow him, follow him.
Jesus says to come follow him
Catching people. *(Have children bring the bridge down and catch the child between their arms.)*

After a few verses, have children trade places to catch the other two children in their groups.

Ask: • **Who can you ask to follow Jesus this week?**

Jesus Heals a Paralyzed Man

God Will Forgive Us

cd2 track 16

Invite your children to join you in a circle on the floor. Tell them that God's forgiveness is like when we erase dirty marks or writing from a piece of paper or chalkboard, then demonstrate it for them to see. Lead your children in singing and doing the motions to "God Will Forgive Us" to the tune of "Jesus Loves Me."

God will forgive us. Yes, we know. *(Pretend to erase a chalkboard.)*

Just because his Word says so. *(Place edges of hands together like a book.)*

We can tell him all our sins *(make praying hands)*

'Cause Jesus is our loving friend. *(Hug yourself.)*

God will forgive us. *(Point up then pretend to erase a chalkboard.)*

God will forgive us.

God will forgive us.

The Bible tells me so. *(Place edges of hands together like a book.)*

I Can Walk!

As you do this finger play with your children, over-dramatize your voice and facial expressions, and lead your children in expressing the different emotions that are being displayed.

Five dear friends *(hold up five fingers)*

But one was crippled. *(Now just hold up one finger, and make it crooked.)*

He couldn't walk, run, or play. *(Walk, run, then jump two fingers up arm.)*

What can we do? How can we help him? *(Shrug shoulders.)*

So on this mat he will not stay. *(Lay two fingers out straight in palm of opposite hand, and shake head "no.")*

Through the roof and down to Jesus on that very special day. *(Make a circle with fingers of one hand, then put two fingers from opposite hand down the hole, open hand, and lay fingers on open palm.)*

Get up, dear friend. Your sins are forgiven! *(Stand fingers up on palm.)*

Now go! Rejoice! Be on your way! *(Walk fingers up arm.)*

Jesus Heals a Paralyzed Man

Mark 2:1-12

Bible Point: Jesus wants to forgive us.

How exciting to have such dear friends that they would not only have the faith to carry you to see Jesus, but would then "raise the roof" for you! As you tell this story, remind your children that not only did Jesus heal the crippled man, but, more important, he forgave his sins. Explain to the children that Jesus told the man that he was forgetting every bad thing that the man had ever done. Remind your children that Jesus wants to forgive their sins, too!

Before you begin, make sure that you have a large beach towel and a paper outline of a man that can be attached to the beach towel. Also, make a square house out of chairs by setting them side by side with the seats facing out. Make the "house" large enough for your class to sit inside but small enough to be crowded while they are in it.

Say: **Jesus had gone to Capernaum and was talking to a group of people in a house.** Choose a child to be Jesus, and place him or her in the house. **The house was very crowded.** Have all but four children go into the house with Jesus. **Everyone was listening to Jesus talk when, all of a sudden, four people came up carrying a crippled man on a mat.** Give the four remaining children the beach towel mat with the paper man placed in the center, and have them carry it to the door of the house. **But there was no way they were going to get in through the door. So they came up with a better plan: They would lower their friend down through the roof.** Help the four children with the mat climb up on the chairs and lower the mat down into the house. Have the children inside the house make room for the mat to be placed on the floor.

The people inside were very surprised! Have the children inside the house make surprised faces.

Ask: • **How would you feel if someone started coming through our ceiling?**

Say: **When Jesus saw them, he did something amazing. He told the crippled man that his sins were forgiven. Well, some of the important teachers who were there didn't like that.** Have children cross their arms and make grouchy faces. **"How can you forgive this man's sins? Do you think that you are God?" they said. Jesus said to the grouchy men, "I will show you that I am the Son of God. I can forgive his sins and tell him to get up and walk." So Jesus turned to the crippled man and said, "Get up, pick up your mat, and go home!"** Have one child pick up the paper man from the mat and pretend to walk him out of the house.

Wow, how exciting for the crippled man!

Ask: • **How would you feel if you could walk all of a sudden?**

• **How do you feel when Jesus forgives the bad things you've done?**

Say: **Jesus loved the man so much that he healed him and said that he forgave all the bad things he had ever done. Jesus forgives the bad things we've done, too.**

If you have a small class and don't have all the characters for the story, choose the main characters first or let some children be more than one character.

Jesus Calms a Storm

A Disciple's Storm Song

track 17

Sing and do the motions to "A Disciple's Storm Song" to the tune of "My Bonnie Lies Over the Ocean."

A boat in the stormy water *(rock side to side)*,
A boat in the stormy sea,
A boat in the stormy water—
Oh, won't someone please help me?

**Jesus, Jesus, I'm so afraid. Please help me, help
me!** *(Hold arms out as if reaching for Jesus.)*
Jesus, Jesus, I'm so afraid. Please help me!
(Hold arms out as if reaching for Jesus.)

Then Jesus said, "Shh!" to the water. *(Hold
index finger to lips.)*
Then Jesus said, "Shh!" to the sea.
Then Jesus said, "Shh!" to the water.
And Jesus said, "Shh!" to me!

**"I will help you whenever you feel afraid,
afraid.** *(Reach arms out as if helping someone.)*
I will help you whenever you feel afraid!"
(Reach arms out as if helping someone.)

Wind and Waves

Many preschoolers are just like the disciples—afraid of storms. Remind your children that Jesus can take away their fears, just as he took away the wind and the waves.

Jesus and his disciples were in a boat. *(Cup
hands together to form a boat and gently rock
back and forth.)*

Jesus took a nap while the boat was afloat. *(Lay
head on hands.)*

All of a sudden, the wind began to blow. *(Blow air.)*
The waves crashed against the boat. Oh, no!
(Clap hands to make crashing sounds.)

Jesus, wake up! Don't let us drown. *(Cup hands
around mouth.)*

**Then Jesus told the wind and the waves to quiet
down.** *(Put index finger to mouth and say, "Shh.")*

**Everything was quiet, and the lake was calm
and clear.** *(Spread hands out in front of you to
show how calm the lake is.)*

Jesus' mighty power was real and very near.
(Show strong arms.)

Jesus Calms the Storm

Mark 4:35-41

Bible Point: Jesus can quiet our fears.

Life for the disciples was never dull! Traveling from place to place, stories to hear, miracles to witness—all because they said "yes" to Jesus. Today's story is no different! It's full of excitement for the disciples and shows the magnitude of Jesus' power. At the end of the story, the disciples were afraid of Jesus' power, since even the wind and waves obeyed him. Explain to the children that we don't have to be afraid of Jesus' power but in awe or surprised by his mighty works.

Before you begin, cut two narrow strips of blue tissue paper for each child. Fill a squirt bottle with water, and set a fan near your story area. You will need to have easy access to the water bottle and fan so that you can turn on the fan when you say "wind," and gently spray the children when you say "waves." Give each child the tissue paper before you begin to teach.

Say: **Our Bible story today is from the book of Mark. It's a story about a mighty storm.**

Ask: • **Have you ever been in a strong storm? What was it like?**

Say: **During the Bible story, you'll get to help me be the storm. When I say "wind," I want you to blow like the wind. When I say "waves," I want you to hold your papers above your heads and gently wave them. When I say "afraid," show me what your face looks like when you're afraid.** Practice a few times, then begin the Bible story.

Jesus had been traveling and teaching during the day. In the evening, Jesus and his disciples got into a boat to go across to the other side of the lake. Jesus was very tired and went to the back of the boat to sleep. All of a sudden, the wind began to blow. Turn the fan on the low setting (if you have controls), and have children blow. **The wind blew harder!** Turn the fan on the medium setting, and have children blow harder. **The wind blew even harder!** Turn the fan on high, and have children blow their very hardest.

Then the waves started splashing into the boat. Have children wave their strips of paper, and use the water bottle to gently spray them. **The disciples were afraid.** Have children show you what they look like when they feel afraid. **The wind and the waves were about to make the boat sink.** Have children blow and wave their papers more. Spray the water into the fan so it sprays out to the children. **Finally, the disciples**

woke Jesus and said, **"Jesus, don't you care that we are about to drown?"** Have children blow and wave their papers. Spray more water into the fan. **Jesus woke up and ordered the wind and the waves to stop.** Stop the fan, and have the children stop blowing and moving their papers.

Everything got quiet, and everything was calm. Have children each put one finger in front of their mouths and say, "Shh." **Then Jesus said, "Why were you afraid?"**

Ask: • **What would you tell Jesus?**

Say: **The disciples couldn't believe their eyes. Even the wind and the waves obeyed Jesus! Everything was still. Everything was quiet. And Jesus had made it all happen. Jesus was like no other person they ever knew. The disciples knew they could believe that Jesus was the Messiah. They knew Jesus calmed their fears and made the storm go away. Jesus was amazing! We know who Jesus is. He is God's Son. We can believe in Jesus to take our fears away and quiet down the things that make us afraid, too.**

Tip From the Trenches

When using props such as a fan or water, things can quickly get wild and out of hand. Before you ever begin, enlist the children's help by explaining that you have a very special story to tell them today but that they must do exactly what you say or it will not work. It can also be helpful to have an extra helper in your room to sit next to a child who seems to be getting overly excited.

Jesus Heals the Blind Man

Jesus Touched and Healed the Blind Man

cd2 track 18

Sing "Jesus Touched and Healed the Blind Man" to the tune of "She'll Be Coming Round the Mountain."

Jesus touched and healed the blind man.
(Touch the person next to you.)
"I can see! Yeehaw!" *(Cover, then uncover eyes.)*
Jesus touched and healed the blind man.
(Touch the person next to you.)
"I can see! Yeehaw!" *(Cover, then uncover eyes.)*

Jesus touched and healed the blind man.
(Touch the person next to you.)
Oh, my Jesus is a kind man!
Jesus touched and healed the blind man.
(Touch the person next to you.)
"I can see! Yeehaw!" *(Cover, then uncover eyes.)*

I Want to See!

How exciting to be able to see all the things you've never seen before! Before doing this finger play, give children an opportunity to share things they would want to see if they were blind.

There once was a blind man who could not see. *(Cover eyes with hands.)*

He cried out to Jesus, "Oh, please help me!"
(Fold hands as if pleading.)

"What do you want?" was Jesus' reply. *(Shrug shoulders.)*

"I want to see grass and trees and the sky!"
(Shield eyes with hand and look around.)

"Go on now; you're healed. Your eyes are just fine. *(Point to eyes.)*

Your faith in me is just the right kind." *(Show two thumbs up.)*

Jesus Heals the Blind Man

Mark 10:46-52

Bible Point: We can believe in Jesus.

Oh, how we take so many things for granted! Have you ever thought about how much you would miss your eyesight if you were like Bartimaeus? How often do we thank Jesus for our gift of sight? As you tell this story, remind your children of their five senses, and take a moment at the end of the Bible story to thank Jesus for the gifts of sight, touch, sound, smell, and taste.

Before you begin, collect pictures of a man and a crowd. Place a large star on each picture, then post the pictures around the room.

As you teach, be sensitive if you have sight-impaired children in your group.

Say: **Today our story is about a very special man. Before we begin, I am going to ask you to use your eyes to find six pictures that I have hidden in this room. Each picture that you are to find has a large star on it.** Give children several minutes to find the pictures, then have them join you back in the story area.

Let's look at the pictures that you have found. Hold up each picture, and have the children tell you what they see in the pictures. **Let's use these pictures to help us tell today's Bible story.** As you tell the story, hold up the appropriate pictures.

Jesus and his disciples were traveling to Jericho. There was a large crowd of people following Jesus. Ask a child to hold up the picture of the crowd. **One of the people in the crowd was a blind man named Bartimaeus.** Ask another child to hold up the picture of the man. **When Bartimaeus realized that Jesus was near, he began to shout, "Jesus, help me!"** Ask half of the children to pretend to be Bartimaeus

and shout, "Jesus, help me!" **The crowd tried to get Bartimaeus to stop shouting.** Have the other half of the children say, "Shh!" and "Be quiet!" **But the more they tried to get Bartimaeus to quiet down, the louder he got. "Jesus, help me!"** Have the two groups repeat their lines at the same time.

Finally, Jesus stopped and called Bartimaeus over to him. The crowd called out to Bartimaeus and told him not to be afraid. They said, "Jesus is calling for you!" When Bartimaeus heard this, he threw off his coat and made his way quickly to Jesus. "What do you want me to do for you?" Jesus asked. Bartimaeus replied, "I want to see!" Have all the children close and cover their eyes. Have the children repeat, "I want to see!" Remind children to keep their eyes closed for just a few more moments.

Then the most amazing thing happened! Jesus said, "You may go; your eyes are all better because you believed in me." Now tell children that they can uncover their eyes. **Right away Bartimaeus could see! Bartimaeus believed in Jesus, and you can believe in Jesus too!**

Tip From the Trenches

When gathering pictures for a story, you have several options. You can look in past curriculum to see if you can find the things you need. Old magazines provide another alternative. Clip art books can also help. You can also draw them yourself! Little children are oblivious to your artistic abilities; they will not care if you draw stick figures or elaborate sketches!

Jesus Feeds Five Thousand

Five Little Loaves and Two Little Fish

cd4 track 19

Sing "Five Little Loaves and Two Little Fish" to the tune of "You Get a Line, and I'll Get a Pole, Honey."

Five little loaves and two little fish, honey. *(Hold up five fingers on one hand, two on the other.)*
Five little loaves and two little fish, babe. *(Repeat motion.)*
Five little loaves and two little fish *(repeat motion),*
In a basket, not a dish. *(Put hands together to form a basket.)*
Honey, oh baby, mine. *(Hug yourself.)*

Jesus took that little boy's lunch, honey. *(Pretend to pat a little boy's head.)*
Jesus took that little boy's lunch, babe. *(Repeat motion.)*
Jesus took that little boy's lunch *(repeat motion)*

Made a meal for the whole bunch. *(Hold hand out with palm up as a plate, grasp an imaginary spoon with other hand, and pretend to eat.)*
Honey, oh baby, mine. *(Hug yourself.)*

Whatcha gonna share in Jesus' name, honey? *(Cross arms over chest, then bring arms out in front of you.)*
Whatcha gonna share in Jesus' name, babe? *(Repeat motion.)*
Whatcha gonna share in Jesus' name? *(Repeat motion.)*
The world may never be the same. *(Grasp arms in a circle over head, and sway side to side.)*
Honey, oh baby, mine. *(Hug yourself.)*

Five Loaves, Two Fish Finger Play

Give each child five round crackers and two fish-shaped crackers, and let them munch their way through this finger play. They will watch as the food disappears and then be reminded at the end that Jesus showed his power and love by making more food so that everyone could be fed. If crackers are not available, let the children pretend to eat the loaves and fish one piece at a time.

Five loaves *(hold up five fingers on one hand),*
Two fish *(hold up two fingers on the opposite hand)—*
Look at all the people. *(Wiggle all ten fingers.)*

Five loaves *(hold up five fingers on one hand),*
Two fish *(hold up two fingers on the other hand)—*
Many hungry people. *(Wiggle all ten fingers.)*

Five loaves *(hold up five fingers on one hand),*
Two fish *(hold up two fingers on the other hand)—*
God fed people. *(Wiggle all ten fingers.)*

Jesus Feeds Five Thousand

John 6:1-15

Bible Point: Jesus can provide for our needs.

Jesus showed his power and his love when he took a young boy's lunch and multiplied it by five thousand. Everyone on the hillside that day went away satisfied. For some, it was only their stomachs that were full. Others had caught a glimpse of the Savior at work, and they knew it. Your little ones need their tummies filled, too, but your greatest work is that which leads a child to an understanding of Christ's love for him or her.

Before you begin, place two fish-shaped crackers and five round crackers in a paper lunch sack. Place the remaining crackers in a breadbasket and set it aside for later. Ask one of the children to carry the sack as you lead the class in this action story. Have children begin the Bible story standing up.

Say: **Let's pretend that we're going to hear Jesus teach. He's way up on a hillside. Let's climb up the hill to Jesus.** Pretend to climb a steep, long hill.

Look at all the people! One, two, three, four…There are too many to count. But where is Jesus? Have children shield their eyes with their hands and look one way, then the other. **There he is, on top of the hill.** Point away.

Shh! Let's sit down and listen to what Jesus is saying. He's telling everyone about God's power and love. He will give them food (pretend to eat) **and clothes** (point to clothes) **and love.** (Hug yourself.)

Jesus has taught all day, and everyone is getting very hungry. Have children rub their tummies and lick their lips. **I think I might even hear some tummies growling.** Have children make growling sounds. **I bet Jesus could hear them too. He wanted to give everyone something to eat, so he sent his disciples in search of food. When they came back to Jesus,**

they said, **"The only food we found is five loaves of bread and two small fishes that a little boy has in his lunch.** Hold up and shake the lunch bag. Let the children see what's in the sack. **He wants to share his lunch, but one lunch isn't enough for all these people."**

Look what Jesus is doing now. He is telling everyone to sit down. Have children join you in sitting down. **He's praying and thanking God for the food. Let's pray with Jesus.** Lead children in saying the following prayer with you: **Thank you, God, for this bread and fish. Amen.**

Jesus' disciples are passing the little boy's lunch around, and all the people are being fed. Pass the lunch bag around and pretend to eat. **Only God can make one small lunch feed lots and lots of people! Look!** Bring out the basket of extra crackers, and let children have some. **There is even food left over!**

Ask: • **Would you have given your only food to Jesus? Why or why not?**

• **What's one way you can thank Jesus for the food he provides for you and your family?**

Say: **Jesus can provide for our needs, and we can thank him through our prayers.**

Jesus Blesses the Children

Jesus Loves Me

cd2 track 20

Play "Jesus Loves Me," and encourage kids to sing and do the actions with you.

Jesus loves me! This I know *(move in a circle, hugging stuffed animals),*
For the Bible tells me so;
Little ones to him belong *(hold animal high in the air),*
They are weak but he is strong. *(Cradle animal in arms.)*

Yes, I'm important! *(Turn around and go in the opposite direction while hugging animals.)*
Yes, I'm important!
Yes, I'm important!
The Bible tells me so.

Jesus Loves Me

In this finger play, the children will review the Bible story and remember that Jesus loves them.

I know Jesus loves me. *(Hug yourself.)*

This is how I know. *(Tap side of head.)*

Jesus let the children come *(motion to come),*

The Bible tells me so. *(Open hands like a book.)*

The disciples growled, "Go away! *(Point away.)*

Don't bother him today. *(Wag finger.)*

He doesn't have time for you,
So run along and play." *(Run fingers up arm.)*

Jesus said, "No, that's not true. *(Wag finger.)*

I want them here with me." *(Point down.)*

One by one, he let them come *(hold up one index finger, then the other)*

And sit upon his knee. *(Pat knees.)*

I know Jesus loves me. *(Hug yourself.)*

This is how I know. *(Tap side of head.)*

Jesus let the children come *(motion to come),*

The Bible tells me so. *(Open hands like a book.)*

Jesus Blesses the Children

Mark 10:13-16

Bible Point: Jesus loves children.

The image of our Lord welcoming children with open arms gives us a glimpse of his tender heart. It was an attitude the disciples apparently didn't share and one which they were sternly rebuked for not having. As you take time with a child today, you will be a step ahead of the disciples and a little closer to the heart of Christ.

Have the children stand up and do the motions as you tell the Bible story.

Say: **The Bible tells us that Jesus loves everyone.** Have kids give high fives to children standing next to them. **Jesus loves tall, strong daddies.** Speak in a deep voice and stand up tall. **He loves kind mommies.** Speak in a soft, sweet voice. **And he loves little children, too.** Speak in a higher voice and crouch down low.

Whenever Jesus was in town, people would walk to see him. Have kids walk in place. **As they walked, the daddies might have said, "Jesus loves me."** Speak in a low voice and stand up tall. **The mommies might have said, "Jesus loves me."** Speak in a soft, sweet voice. **The little children might have said, "Jesus loves me, too."** Speak in a higher voice and crouch down low.

They would sit and listen to Jesus tell about God. Have kids sit down. **They would stand and watch him make a sick person well.** Have kids stand up. **Sometimes they just wanted Jesus to touch them and tell them they were special to God.** Have kids pat a friend's shoulder.

One day, many children were coming to Jesus. Have kids come in close to you. **This made the disciples mad.** Have kids put their hands on their hips and look mad.

"Go away," they growled. Growl, "Go away!" **They didn't think Jesus wanted the children there. They thought he was too busy.** Have kids walk around the room telling everyone, "Go away. Jesus is too busy." **But Jesus said, "Don't send them away. See how they believe in me? Let them come. I want them here with me."** Form a group hug.

As they walked home that day, the daddies might have said, "Jesus loves me." Speak in a low voice and stand up tall. **The mommies might have said, "Jesus loves me."** Speak in a soft, sweet voice. **The little children might have said, "Jesus loves me, too."** Speak in a higher voice and crouch down low.

Ask: • **Why do you think Jesus wanted the children to come to him?**

• **What would you tell Jesus if you could sit on his lap?**

Say: **Jesus wanted the disciples to see that children were important to him and that he loved them. Always remember that Jesus loves children.**

This is a good day for hugs. Use your greeting and goodbye times as opportunities to show your kids that you love them.

Jesus Clears the Temple

Worship God

cd2 track 21

Sing "Worship God" to the tune of "Old MacDonald Had a Farm." After singing the song a few times, let your children think of other ways to praise, such as clapping, stomping, jumping, or dancing. When you sing, "Praise with a…" let your children demonstrate their unique ways to worship God and praise him.

Worship God and God alone! (*Point up.*)
Show God all your love. (*Cross arms over chest.*)
Worship God and God alone! (*Point up.*)
Praise his name above. (*Raise both hands.*)

Praise with a shout! (*Cup hands to mouth.*)
Praise with a cheer! (*Punch fist in air.*)
Show God that we love him here! (*Cross arms over chest.*)

Worship God and God alone! (*Point up.*)
Show him all your love. (*Raise hands.*)

In God's House

Those who reduced the Temple to a market were an example of the wrong things to do with God's house. In this finger play, children will think about the right things to do. Have your children begin by standing.

When I'm in God's house, I pray (*raise arms over head with hands together to form a pointed roof, then make praying hands*),

And this is what I say,
"Jesus, thank you for my church. I'm glad I'm here today." (*Raise arms over head with hands together to form a pointed roof.*)

When I'm in God's house, I sing (*raise arms over head with hands together to form a pointed roof, then pretend to conduct*),

And this is how it sounds (*sing the following line*):
"Jesus loves me! This I know, for the Bible tells me so."
When I'm in God's house, I sit. (*Raise arms over head with hands together to form a pointed roof, then sit down.*)

My teachers tell me of God's love, and how he cares for me. (*Hug yourself.*)

When I'm in God's house, I know (*raise arms over head with hands together to form a pointed roof, then tap side of head*),

That God is here with me.
I will pray (*make praying hands*)

And sing (*pretend to conduct*)

And worship God (*clap hands*),

For this makes God happy with me. *(Hug yourself.)*

Jesus Clears the Temple

John 2:13-22

Bible Point: God wants us to worship him.

God's house was made for worship. When it became a marketplace, Jesus said, "That's enough. No more!" The offense reflected a low regard for the things of God and, ultimately, for God himself. Teach your children to honor God first and treat their church building with respect.

Before you begin, divide the children into cows, sheep, doves, and sellers with jingling coins. Let the animals move about on their hands and knees. Give each of the sellers a few coins to shake inside resealable plastic bags.

Say: **It was a special day at the Temple church. People were coming to pray and to show God that they were sorry for their sins. As Jesus came close to the Temple, he could hear the sounds of animals.**

Cows were mooing. Point to the "cows," and have them "moo." **Sheep were baaing.** Point to the "sheep," and have them "baa." **Doves were cooing.** Point to the "doves," and have them "coo." **There was also the sound of sellers jingling their money.** Point to the "sellers," and have them jingle their coins.

"These are not the sounds of people praying to God," said Jesus. "These are sounds of people buying and selling things."

Men were selling cows. Point to the cows, and have them "moo." **Men were selling sheep.** Point to the sheep, and have them "baa." **Men were selling doves.** Point to the doves, and have them "coo." **The sellers were taking extra money for themselves. The**

sound of their jingling coins could be heard all across the Temple. Point to the sellers, and have them jingle their coins.

Jesus said, "God's house should not be a store. All of these things must go!"

He chased the cows away. Point to the cows, and have them "moo" and run away. **He chased the sheep away.** Point to the sheep, and have them "baa" and run away. **He chased the doves away.** Point to the doves, and have them "coo" and "fly" away. **He chased the sellers with their jingling coins away.** Point to the sellers, and have them jingle their coins and run away.

Gather the children, and have them sit down in front of you on the floor.

Say: **Jesus loved God's house. He knew God was not pleased that men were selling things there instead of worshipping him.**

Jesus taught us that God's house is for singing, praying, and learning about God. Let's thank God for our church where we can worship him. Remind children that God wants us to worship him, and then thank God for your church building.

If the children are not familiar with the word *Temple*, explain that the Temple was where Jesus went to worship God—it is a Bible-times church.

Jesus Notices a Widow's Giving

God Loves a Cheerful Giver

Have the children sit down in a circle. Give each child a sandwich-size resealable bag of snack crackers or small candies. Choose one child to be the "Giver." Have the Giver walk around the inside of the circle, giving a piece of his or her snack to each of his or her friends while you sing "God Loves a Cheerful Giver" to the tune of "The Bear Went Over the Mountain." Repeat the singing game until all the children have had a turn to be the Giver.

God loves a cheerful giver.
God loves a cheerful giver.
God loves a cheerful giver,
And that means he loves me.
And that means he loves me.

And that means he loves me.
God loves a cheerful giver.
God loves a cheerful giver.
God loves a cheerful giver,
And that means he loves me!

Little Coins for Jesus

I'll share a little secret that's hardly ever told. *(Place hands around mouth and pretend to whisper.)*

Some people think the way to get is to grab and hold. *(Pretend to grab the air.)*

But God loves a cheerful giver who gives his love and gold. *(Hold hands out.)*

If we start now, we'll learn to give as we're growing old. *(Pretend to lean on a cane.)*

Jesus Notices a Widow's Giving

Mark 12:41-44

Bible Point: God wants us to give what we have.

While it may have appeared slight in comparison to others, the poor widow's offering was great in the eyes of God. The gift of caring for your children may seem like a small thing, but it is also great in the eyes of God. Thank you for giving God's love to your children. Remember that you are as valuable to God as the widow's gift.

Make two copies of the "Money, Money" handout (p. 158) for each child. Cut out the coins, and give each child ten paper coins. Place a large aluminum bowl in the center of the circle.

Say: **The Bible tells us that Jesus was sitting at a place in the Temple where people brought their gifts to God. One by one, the rich people brought their coins and dropped them into the money box. As the coins fell in, they made a lot of noise.** Have children count and set aside two coins. Then let each child take a turn slowly dropping the rest of his or her coins into the bowl. As children drop their coins, drop in real coins so that they make a lot of noise.

Jesus watched as the people gave money to God. They thought they were pretty good for being rich and having lots of money to give to God. After all, they had lots and lots more coins at home.

Jesus continued to watch and listen as coin after coin was dropped into the money box.

Then Jesus saw a very poor woman walk up to the money box. She didn't have very much money at all. She had only two coins and nothing more at home.

Ask: • **What would you do if you had only two coins?**

• **What do you think the poor woman did with her coins?**

Say: **The poor woman had only two coins to give to God. She didn't have any more money at home. Even though it wasn't much, she dropped the coins into the money box. They barely made a sound.** Let children take turns dropping their last two coins into the bowl.

Jesus watched as the woman gave her money to God. He heard the tiny sound it made as it dropped into the money box. And Jesus knew that the woman was giving all the money she had in the world to God. He told the disciples that this poor woman's gift was worth more than all the money that the rich people had given because it was everything she had.

God wants us to give gifts to him too. Little gifts can be big when they are given to God. He sees what you give, and he says "thank you."

Ask: • **What do you have that you can give to God?**

Say: **God wants us to give what we have.**

Jesus Teaches His Disciples to Pray

This Is How We Should Pray

Create two groups of children, and lead them in echoing the lines as they sing "This Is How We Should Pray" to the tune of "Everybody Ought to Know."

This is how we should pray. (*First group sings*)
This is how we should pray (*second group echoes*):
Dear Father in heaven (*first group sings*),
Your name is holy. (*Second group sings.*)

He is always listening to me. (*All together.*)
I will talk to God today. (*All together.*)

He is always right beside me. (*All together.*)
He hears every word I say. (*All together.*)

This is how we should pray. (*First group sings.*)
This is how we should pray (*second group echoes*):
Dear Father in heaven (*first group sings*),
Your name is holy. (*Second group sings.*)

Two Praying Men

Before you begin, give each child two Bugle snacks to place on their thumbs. With their left and right thumbs, the children will finger play two men who prayed. One man's prayer pleased God, but the other man's did not.

This man stood up very tall and shouted out a prayer (*wiggle first thumb*):
"Oh, dear God, please watch me now as I'm giving you a call."
This other man bowed his head down low and closed his eyes real tight. (*Wiggle second thumb.*)
He whispered a quiet prayer to God: "Be with me through the night."

This man said, "I love you, God." (*Wiggle second thumb.*)
This man, he did not. (*Wiggle first thumb.*)
This man's prayer made God happy. (*Wiggle second thumb.*)
This man's prayer did not. (*Wiggle first thumb.*)

Jesus Teaches His Disciples to Pray

Matthew 6:5-13

Bible Point: God wants us to talk to him.

Jesus knew the valuable lesson of talking to God and gave his disciples a pattern to follow. As you teach your children ways they can talk to God, you are helping them begin their daily relationship with their Father, God.

Before you begin, have two Bugle snacks for each child to use during the Bible story. Ask kids to sit together in a circle as you tell the following story.

Say: **When you were very little, you learned to walk. You also learned to talk. Now that you are older, you are learning many more things.**

Ask: • **What can you do that you couldn't do before?**

Say: **One of the most important things you can learn is how to pray. When we pray, we are talking to God.**

Ask: • **What are some of the things you tell God?**

Tell your children to listen carefully for the word *pray*. Each time they hear you say "pray," they are to fold their hands as if praying.

Say: **Jesus taught his disciples how to** *pray* (make praying hands) **by first telling them what they should not do.**

Jesus said, "When you *pray* (make praying hands)**, don't keep looking around to see if someone is watching you. You should never** *pray* (make praying hands) **just because you want others to look at you. Some people** *pray* (make praying hands, then shout the following) **in a loud voice for a long time just so someone will notice them.** Have the children yell, "Hello, God! I'm talking to you!" **Praying loudly is OK, but not when you want everyone to look at you. That's not the right way to** *pray*.**"** Make praying hands.

Jesus taught the disciples the right way to *pray*. Make praying hands. **He said they could say quiet prayers.** Have the children whisper, "Hi, God. I'm glad you hear me." **Jesus said, "When you** *pray* (make praying hands)**, go to a quiet place where no one is watching. Sit down and tell God that you love him.** Have children place their hands in their laps and say, "I love you, God."

Jesus said to tell God what they're thankful for. Let each child name one thing he or she is thankful for. Have kids take turns saying, "Thank you, God, for…" **Ask God to take care of you.** Have children say, "God, please take care of me today." **Ask God to forgive you if you do something wrong. Ask him to help you do what is right.** Have kids say, "Dear Jesus, please forgive me and help me do what's right."

God hears what you *pray* (make praying hands) **and listens to everything you tell him. We can** *pray* (make praying hands) **quiet prayers every day. We know that we can talk to God anytime and anywhere.**

Ask: • **Where are some places you can pray?**

Say: **We can** *pray* (make praying hands) **in the house or in the car or when we're playing outside. We can** *pray* (make praying hands) **out loud, and we can** *pray* (make praying hands) **with other people, but God will also hear us when we** *pray* (make praying hands) **quietly or all by ourselves. God wants us to talk to him anywhere and at any time.**

Zacchaeus Sees Jesus

Did You Ever See Zacchaeus?

Have your children stand up and sing "Did You Ever See Zacchaeus?" to the tune of "Did You Ever See a Lassie?"

Did you ever see Zacchaeus,
Zacchaeus, Zacchaeus?
Did you ever see Zacchaeus,
Way up in a tree? *(Look up, shielding eyes with hand.)*

He looked 'round for Jesus *(scan around with hand over eyes)*
Then climbed up to see him *(make climbing motions)*;
Did you ever see Zacchaeus,
Way up in a tree?

Jesus saw Zacchaeus,
Zacchaeus, Zacchaeus.
Jesus saw Zacchaeus *(look up, shielding eyes with hand)*
Way up in that tree. *(Point up.)*

Zacchaeus come down now;
I'm coming to your house.
Jesus saw Zacchaeus *(look up, shielding eyes with hand)*
Way up in that tree. *(Point up.)*

I May Be Short, But God Loves Me

This finger play will help your children understand that God loves everyone, no matter how big or small or where they come from. We can all rejoice that we're loved by God.

I may be short *(pat the air)*,

But God loves me. *(Hug yourself.)*

Just like Zacchaeus up in the tree *(point up)*,

God loves all people
From east to west. *(Spread one arm out, then the other.)*

Following Jesus is the very best! Yeah! *(Raise hands and cheer.)*

Zacchaeus Sees Jesus

Luke 19:1-10

Bible Point: Be kind and show God's love to everyone.

Zacchaeus may have been a short man, but he was a very important man in his community. As a tax collector, he was feared and disliked. When Jesus chose to spend time with Zacchaeus, some people were outraged. Because of Jesus' caring and kindness, Zacchaeus gave his heart and life to Jesus. Through this lesson, we can teach our children that they can be kind and show God's love to everyone.

The children will enjoy acting out this story with you in a Follow the Leader style. As you read this story, do the motions, and have the children follow you in a single-file line.

Say: **Jesus was walking through the town of Jericho.** Start marching around the room. **All the people came out to see him.** Stop and place a hand across your brow as if looking in the distance. **One man named Zacchaeus was too short to see over all the people.** Jump up and down as if trying to see over people.

The people did not like Zacchaeus because he had cheated them out of money. Cup your hands around your mouth and say, "Boo! Hiss!" **Since no one would let him see Jesus, Zacchaeus climbed up high in a tree to see Jesus pass by.** Pretend to climb up a tree.

Jesus stopped and told Zacchaeus to come down because he wanted to spend the day with him. Wave your arm and say, "Come on down!" **As Jesus and Zacchaeus walked to Zacchaeus' house,**

the people told Jesus he shouldn't be with Zacchaeus.** Start walking again, shake your finger, and say, "Don't go, don't go!"

Zacchaeus got to spend a long time getting to know Jesus. Jesus was kind and showed God's love to him even when everyone else was mean. Put your hands around a friend's shoulder. **Zacchaeus thanked Jesus for being kind to him and said that he would no longer cheat the people and would give back all the money he had taken.** Pretend to give friends money.

Jesus said he came to show God's love to everyone, whether they were nice or mean. Jesus saw that Zacchaeus' heart had changed. Zacchaeus had now decided to be nice to people and not take more taxes from them than what he was supposed to. Hug your neighbor.

Ask: • **How did Jesus show God's love to Zacchaeus?**

• **How can you show God's love to people who are mean?**

• **Who do you know that needs to see God's love?**

Say: **Be kind and show God's love to everyone, just as Jesus was kind and showed God's love to Zacchaeus.**

Tip From the Trenches

Young preschoolers may not understand why a tax collector was so hated in Jesus' society, but they do understand when they have been cheated or treated unfairly. Remind them of how they feel when someone does something wrong to them. This is why the people disliked Zacchaeus.

Jesus Tells the Parable of the Lost Son

My God ● cd2 track 25

Sing "My God" to the tune of "My God Is So Great."

My God is so good. (*Give thumbs up.*)
God forgives me and loves me (*hug yourself*),
Even if I do something that's wrong. (*Give thumbs down.*)
My God is so good. (*Give thumbs up.*)
God forgives me and loves me (*hug yourself*),
Even if I do something that's wrong. (*Give thumbs down.*)

God loves me always. (*Point toward the sky.*)
God forgives me each day,
And that is why I love him so. (*Hug yourself.*)
My God is so good. (*Give thumbs up.*)
God forgives me and loves me (*hug yourself*),
Even if I do something that's wrong. (*Give thumbs down.*)

Tale of Two Sons ●

Your children will enjoy retelling the Bible story with this finger play.

There was a man who had two boys. (*Hold up two fingers.*)

One saved his money, the other bought toys. (*Put one hand out, then the other.*)

One son went far away (*place hand on forehead*)

And only lived to laugh and play. (*Make a funny laugh.*)
Soon his money all ran out. (*Hold out both hands, palms up.*)

He was cold and hungry, there was no doubt. (*Cross arms and shiver.*)

Going home was his only choice. (*Walk fingers up arm.*)

When his father saw him, he did rejoice. (*Clap hands.*)

"Our son was lost, but now he's found!" (*Put out one hand, palm up, then the other.*)

For both sons, love did abound. (*Hug yourself.*)

The Lost Son

Luke 15:11-32

Bible Point: We can rejoice because God always loves us.

Children will enjoy acting out this story. As you read the story, do the motions indicated, and have your children follow your lead.

Say: **There was a man who had two sons.** Hold up two fingers. **He loved both of his sons very much. One son liked being at home, so he kept his father's money there. The other son wanted to take all of his father's money and see the world. So his father sadly agreed and said goodbye to his son.** Wave goodbye and start walking in place.

He had so much money that he could do anything he wanted—and he did.

Ask: • **What would you do if you had lots and lots of money?**

Say: **Pretty soon he had spent all his money on bad things.** Pretend to give dollar bills to all your friends. **Soon he had no place to live.** Shake your head, then lay your head on your hands. **Soon he had no food to eat.** Shake head, then pretend to put something in your mouth. **He was very cold and hungry.** Hug yourself and shiver.

One day, as he thought about his home, the son remembered that his father's servants weren't hungry or cold. The son remembered that his father took care of them and made sure they were warm and had good meals, and he wondered if his father would let him come home after he had done such bad things.

Ask: • **Do you think the father will let his son come home? Why or why not?**

Say: **The son decided that he would try to go home and work as a servant for his father.** Start walking in place again. **While the son was walking down the road to his home, his father saw him coming from far away in the distance.** Shield your eyes with your hand and look far away.

Ask: • **How do you think the father felt when he saw his son coming home?**

• **How do you feel when you see your best friend coming to your house?**

Say: **The father was so happy to see his son coming that he had his servants prepare a huge feast so they could have a great big party and celebrate the son's return.** Raise your hands in the air and say, "Woo-hoo!"

The first son wondered why his father had never given him a big party. He had never run away. He had always done good things and obeyed his father.

The father told his first son that they would always have each other to love, but right now they were going to celebrate the other son's return by having a great big party to remember that the son who was once lost came back home. Remember that we can rejoice because God always loves us like the father in the Bible story. It was time to rejoice! Jump up and down and yell, "Hurray!"

Tip From the Trenches

Before telling the story, talk with the children about things that were special to them that they may have lost and then found again so that they might understand the joy the father had in seeing his son return home.

Jesus Walks on Water

Jesus Walked on Water

cd2 track 26

Sing "Jesus Walked on Water" to the tune of "Did You Ever See a Lassie?" As you sing the song, have your children stand up and pretend to walk and balance themselves on water.

Jesus walked upon the water,
The water, the water.
Jesus walked upon the water.
He is God's Son.

Peter walked upon the water,
The water, the water.
Peter walked upon the water.
He had faith in God.

Water Walk

By keeping our eyes on the Lord, we can stay afloat in any circumstance.

Water walk and stay afloat (*make wave motions*)**;**

Jesus wants Peter to climb out of the boat. (*Cup one hand, then place two fingers from opposite hand inside, and then have them jump out.*)

Water walk and stay afloat (*make wave motions*)**;**

Peter turned, "Hey, look at me! Take note!"
    (*Point to yourself.*)

Water walk and stay afloat (*make wave motions*)**;**

Keep your eyes on Jesus 'cause he's our lifeboat. (*Point to eyes, then point up.*)

Jesus Walks on Water

Matthew 14:22-33

Bible Point: Jesus will take care of you.

When a storm arose suddenly in the night, catching the disciples off guard in their boat, they were afraid for their lives. When they looked up and saw Jesus walking across the waves, they became even more frightened. When Peter tried to walk out to Jesus, the moment he took his eyes off him, he began to sink. Jesus was able to rescue him and get them both back in the boat. This lesson will help teach your children that by keeping our eyes on the Lord, we can be assured that he will care for us.

Children will enjoy listening to and helping you make the sound effects for this story. Read the story, prompting the children as to when they are to help with the sound effects.

Say: **After feeding five thousand people, Jesus sent his disciples across the lake in a boat so that he could have time to pray.** Pretend to row a boat and say, "Swish, swish, swish."

As night came and the disciples were still out on the water, a big storm started to blow. Make wave motions with your arms and say, "Woo, woo!" **The disciples were very afraid!** Cup your hands around your mouth and say, "Help us, help us!"

The storm began to blow harder. Make wave motions with your arms and blow harder, saying, "Woo, woo!" even louder. Gradually get louder and louder. **Jesus saw the disciples in the boat way out on the lake.** Shield your eyes with your hand, and pretend to look far away.

Ask: • **How do you think you might feel if you were on the boat?**

• **What would you pray to God?**

Say: **The disciples were very scared, and Jesus knew that.**

Ask: • **How do you think Jesus might go help them?**

Say: **Jesus began to walk out toward them across the water. It was amazing! His feet floated! He walked right on top of the water!** Pretend to walk in place, balancing and saying, "Swoosh, swoosh,

swoosh." Pretend that the waves are getting higher and higher. Say, "Splish, splash, splish, splash." **All of a sudden, the disciples saw Jesus coming. "But how could he be walking on top of the water?" they said. This made them feel very afraid.** Hold up your hands and say, "Who could it be, who could it be?"

Ask: • **What do you do when you're afraid?**

Say: **When Jesus came closer to them, he told them that they didn't need to be afraid anymore because he was with them. Jesus was there to take care of them.**

Peter said to Jesus, "If it's really you, Jesus, let me walk on the water with you." So Jesus told brave Peter to come out of the boat and walk to him. Pretend to get out of the boat and walk to Jesus saying, "Splish, splash, splish, splash." **As long as Peter kept looking straight at Jesus, his feet floated on top of the water too. But uh-oh! Peter turned to look at his other friends in the boat, and guess what happened! Peter began to sink.** Say, "Save me! Kersplash!"

Ask: • **What would you do if you were sinking?**

Say: **Right away, Peter turned to Jesus for help. Jesus was already reaching out his hand to Peter to bring him up out of the water. Jesus took care of Peter when he was sinking and put him safely back in the boat with the other disciples.** Say, "Woo!" and relax.

Just then the storm became quiet. Put your index finger up to your lips and say, "Shhh!" **That's when all the disciples knew Jesus really was the Son of God and would take care of them.** (Jump and shout, "Alleluia!")

Jesus Explains Eternal Life to Nicodemus

Life in Heaven

cd2 track 27

Sing "Life in Heaven" to the tune of "Oh, Dear! What Can the Matter Be?"

Dear God, give us life in heaven! *(Fold hands and bow head.)*

Dear God, give us life in heaven! *(Fold hands and bow head.)*

Dear God, give us life in heaven! *(Fold hands and bow head.)*

In Jesus' name, amen! *(Throw hands up in the air.)*

Born Again From the Inside Out

This finger play will help the children learn that when we're born again, we are changed on the inside, not on the outside.

I'm one of God's little children. *(Point to yourself.)*

He loves me, oh, so much. *(Hug yourself.)*

I want to live forever with him *(spread arms out wide)*

And feel his loving touch. *(Hug yourself.)*

He tells me in the Bible *(place hands together like a book),*

I must be born again. *(Hold hands out, palms up.)*

He changes me from the inside out. *(Point to yourself, then away.)*

I praise him and say, "Amen!" *(Clap hands, then shout "Amen!")*

Jesus Explains Eternal Life to Nicodemus

John 3:1-21

Bible Point: We can be born again.

Nicodemus may have been a respected Jewish teacher, but he was having a hard time understanding how he could have eternal life. Your preschoolers may not understand the spiritual concept of rebirth, but they do understand the concept of new birth—something fresh and new. With this lesson, help your children understand that all that is required of us is to believe that Jesus is the Son of God and the forgiver of our sins.

Set out a bowl of muddy water, a basin of clean water, a bar of soap, paper towels, and baby powder. Tell children they will need to shout, "You can be born again!" when you direct them to. Practice shouting a few times before you tell the story.

Say: **There was once a man, named Nicodemus, who was a Jewish teacher. Some people say that he might have been afraid to be seen with Jesus, so he sneaked out of his house when it was dark.** Have the children stand up, hide their faces as with a cape, and pretend to sneak around the room. After about a minute, direct the children back to you.

When he found Jesus, Nicodemus asked him about being God's Son and the miracles he had performed. He also asked Jesus how he could get into the kingdom of heaven.

Ask: • **How do you think you can get into heaven?**

Say: **Jesus told him that to enter God's kingdom, he must be born again.** Have kids say, "You can be born again!"

Nicodemus said, "What do you mean, born again? Certainly I can't go back into my mother's tummy and become a baby again." Have kids say, "You can be born again!"

Ask: • **How would you feel if you were a tiny, little baby again?**

• **Do you think Jesus was talking about shrinking down into your mommy's tummy? Why or why not?**

Say: **Babies are something fresh and new. Jesus was talking about us becoming fresh and new. When we do bad things, it's kind of like when we get all dirty.**

Bring out the bowl of muddy water, basin of clean water, bar of soap, paper towels, and baby powder. Invite the children to come up, feel the muddy water, and observe how it gets them dirty. Remind them that the bad things we do are like the muddy water and we need to be made fresh and new. Have the children wash their hands with the clean water and soap. Then have them dry their hands, and sprinkle a small amount of baby powder on their hands.

Say: **When we believe that Jesus is God's Son and ask him to take away the bad things we do, he makes us fresh and new. We start all over being clean again. That's what Jesus was trying to tell Nicodemus that dark night. But Nicodemus still had a hard time understanding how he could be born again.** Have kids say, "You can be born again!"

Jesus told Nicodemus that in order to get into heaven, we have to be born through the Holy Spirit, when we believe that Jesus is God's Son and can forgive us. Have kids say, "You can be born again!"

Then Jesus told Nicodemus that God loves everyone here on earth so much that he sent Jesus to be born and die for our sins. Now we can have the bad things we do washed away by Jesus, then someday we'll live forever in heaven with him. Jesus wants us to believe in him and be born again. Have kids say, "You can be born again!"

Jesus Talks With a Samaritan Woman

cd2 track 28

Jesus Satisfies

Sing "Jesus Satisfies" to the tune of "London Bridge."

Jesus fills our empty cup *(hold out hands, palms up)*,
Empty cup, empty cup.
Jesus fills our empty cup *(pretend to pour from one hand into the other)*
With living water.

We won't be thirsty anymore *(shake head "no")*,
Anymore, anymore.
We won't be thirsty anymore—
Jesus satisfies! *(Smile and rub tummy.)*

Living Water

This little finger play will help your children learn that Jesus' message of love and forgiveness is for all of us. We only need to accept it.

Jesus has some living water. *(Pretend to take a drink.)*

He offers it to me. *(Point to yourself.)*

Believe in him with all my heart *(draw a heart on chest)*,

I'll never be thirsty. *(Hold hands out, palms up.)*

Jesus Talks With a Samaritan Woman

John 4:5-42

Bible Point: Jesus loves everyone.

Just the simple fact that Jesus, a Jewish man, would take the time to speak to a Samaritan woman spoke volumes of his love and acceptance of all people. He was demonstrating to his disciples that God offers everyone his love and salvation. With this lesson, you can teach your children that Jesus' message of love and forgiveness is for everyone.

Before you begin, bring in some bottled water with a new label put on it that says, "Living Water."

The children will enjoy acting out this story. Read the story and do the motions while the children follow your lead. Begin by walking around the room with the children following behind you.

Say: **Jesus had been on a long walk in the hot sun.** Walk in place and pretend to be very hot. **Jesus was very tired. "I'm thirsty," he said as he came upon a woman at a well.** Pretend to be really thirsty. **The woman looked surprised that Jesus would talk to her.** Look surprised.

"Would you like for me to give you a drink?" she asked Jesus.

"I could give you some living water," Jesus told the woman.

"But you don't even have a bucket and rope. Where would you get it?" the woman asked.

"If you drink this water in the well, you will be thirsty again and need to come back for more water," Jesus said. "But when you drink my living water, you will have eternal life. I know all about you, and I have come so that you can live forever with God, my Father." Give each child a cup, and then pour some of your "living water" in it.

The woman then went into the town and told everyone she saw that she had met God's Son who came to save them. Walk around telling everyone, "Jesus loves you," then sit down.

Jesus loves everyone. Jesus came to share his living water with everyone who would receive it, including the woman at the well that day.

Jesus' friends wondered to whom Jesus had been talking. He told them that they were to go out and tell everyone how they could live forever with God. Let's practice doing that right now. Stand up and walk around again, telling three other friends that Jesus loves them. Then sit back down.

Now all the people will have a chance to believe.

Ask: • **Who would you like to tell that Jesus loves them?**

Say: **Jesus loves you, and Jesus loves everyone in the world. He wants them to know him too.**

The concept of Jesus' living water may be hard for young children to grasp. Let them know that Jesus' water was not real water but the message of eternal life that he had to share with the woman and all people.

Jesus Tells About a Good Samaritan

The Good Samaritan

cd2 track 29

Sing "The Good Samaritan" to the tune of "The Farmer in the Dell."

The man laid in the road. (*Place index finger on open palm of opposite hand.*)

The man laid in the road. (*Repeat motion.*)

"Oh me, oh my, don't pass me by." (*Place hands on cheeks and shake head "no."*)

The man laid in the road. (*Place index finger on open palm of opposite hand.*)

A priest walked right by. (*Walk fingers on open palm of opposite hand.*)

A Levite walked right by. (*Repeat motion.*)

"Oh me, oh my, don't pass me by." (*Place hands on cheeks and shake head "no."*)

They both walked right by. (*Walk fingers on open palm of opposite hand.*)

The good Samaritan helped. (*Brush hand across open palm of opposite hand.*)

The good Samaritan helped. (*Repeat motion.*)

Hooray, hooray, he saved the day. (*Place hands on cheeks and shake head "no."*)

The good Samaritan helped. (*Brush hand across open palm of opposite hand.*)

Show His Love

Lead your children in the following finger play to help reinforce the Bible story.

When asked who we should be kind to (*place finger on side of head*),

Jesus had one reply (*hold up one finger*):

"Love your neighbor as yourself (*hold hands out, palms up*)

And the Lord you will glorify." (*Smile and raise hands in praise.*)

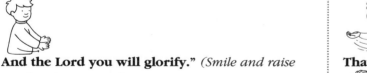

It doesn't matter where you live (*hold hands out, palms up*)

Or who you seem to know (*shake a friend's hand*),

God wants us all to help each other. (*Sweep hand out in front of you.*)

That's how his love we show. (*Hug yourself.*)

Jesus Tells About a Good Samaritan

Luke 10:25-37

Bible Point: Jesus wants us to love everyone.

When asked to explain the phrase "love your neighbor as yourself," Jesus told the story of the Jew who was attacked on his way to Jericho. After being badly hurt, he was passed up by two men before a Samaritan, who was a despised man, stopped to help him and used his own money to care for him. As you teach your children to love everyone, you will also be teaching them that we are all valuable in God's eyes. Jesus wants us to love everyone as he does.

As you read this story, act out the motions, and encourage the children to do the motions with you.

Say: **When Jesus told the people they were to love their neighbors as themselves, someone asked him just who our neighbor is. Jesus then told a story about a type of man that the Jewish people wouldn't talk to because he was from Samaria, a place nearby.**

One day a Jewish man went traveling and walking down the road. Have the children stand, then lead them around in a circle a couple of times. Have the children sit down in the circle. Choose a child to be the Jewish man and stand in the center of the circle. **Some bad men came, took all his money, and left him badly hurt on the ground.** Invite two or three other children to pretend to take things from the "Jewish man" in the center and then sit back down in the circle. Have the Jewish man lie down in the center of the circle.

One very important man walked by and saw him lying there. He was afraid that he might get hurt also, so he continued walking by the man. Choose a child to walk around the inside of the circle, looking at the Jewish man and looking afraid. Then have him or her rejoin the sitting children.

A second man walked by the poor hurt man lying on the ground. He was so afraid that he walked way over on the other side of the road so he wouldn't be near the hurt man. Choose another child to walk around the outside of the circle, looking at the Jewish man and looking afraid. Then have him or her rejoin the sitting children.

Finally, a Samaritan man came along, saw the man hurt and lying on the ground, and wanted to help him. He even knew that Jewish men didn't like him because he was a Samaritan, but he was a kind man and wanted to help him anyway. Choose a child to walk around the outside of the circle first and then go inside the circle, looking at the Jewish man. Have the child kneel down next to the Jewish man and pretend to fix his hurt arms and legs.

The good Samaritan bandaged all the Jewish man's hurt places, put him on his donkey, and took him to an inn where he could get some rest. Invite another child to pretend to be a donkey, and have the Jewish man sit on the "donkey's" back for a short ride to the pretend inn.

The good Samaritan gave the innkeeper some money to take care of the man and promised to pay the cost of whatever he needed. Thank all your actors and actresses and then have them rejoin the circle.

Ask: • **When have you been nice to someone who was mean to you?**

• **Who can you be extra nice to this week?**

Say: **Jesus told the Jewish people that the good Samaritan was the true neighbor. They should treat everyone as the Samaritan man treated the hurt man. Jesus wants us to love everyone, even if they seem different from us.**

Encourage the children to talk about times they have been able to help somebody or someone has been able to help them.

Jesus Enters Jerusalem

Hosanna to Our Savior

cd2 track 30

Sing "Hosanna to Our Savior" to the tune of "Ten Little Indians."

Here comes Jesus riding on a donkey. *(Pretend to ride a donkey.)*

Here comes Jesus riding on a donkey.

Here comes Jesus riding on a donkey—

Hosanna to our Savior! *(Raise hands above head and sway back and forth.)*

Spread palm branches down before him. *(Pretend to lay down coats and palm branches.)*

Spread palm branches down before him.

Spread palm branches down before him—

Hosanna to our Savior! *(Raise hands above head and sway back and forth.)*

Hosanna, the Lord Is Come

Riding a donkey through Jerusalem he came *(pretend to ride a donkey),*

With everyone shouting and calling his name. *(Cup hands around mouth.)*

"Hosanna, Hosanna," came the crowd's cry *(raise hands over head),*

Waving their palms to praise the Lord on high. *(Wave arms over head.)*

Jesus Enters Jerusalem

Matthew 21:1-11; Luke 19:28-40

Bible Point: Jesus wants us to celebrate him as King.

It seems ironic that just a week before Jesus was to be crucified, all of Jerusalem was praising him and declaring that he was the King of glory. Here we find Jesus entering the city on a donkey, being praised and exalted by all who see him. Through this story, you and your children can praise God, just as the people of Jerusalem did.

Before you begin, cut twelve 1x12-inch strips of green construction paper, and tie a piece of yarn around one end to hold them together. This will be your palm frond. Then make one for each of your children.

Give each child a palm frond. As you read the following Bible story, act out the motions, and have the children follow your lead and wave their palm fronds to celebrate Jesus' Triumphal Entry.

Say: **Jesus and his friends were walking to Jerusalem.** Have the children stand up and walk around the room a couple of times, anticipating getting to the city.

Ask: • **What might you talk about on a long walk with Jesus?**

Say: **Jesus sent a couple of his disciple friends ahead of him into the city to find a special donkey for Jesus to ride.** Have children shield their eyes with their hands, then send them around the room for about thirty seconds, looking for a donkey to ride. Encourage kids to use their imagination and find something that they could pretend is a donkey. Some might find a chair, a riding toy, or a class friend.

Jesus' friends found the donkey and brought it to Jesus to ride. Have children pull their "donkeys" to the sides of your story area and then sit down.

Ask: • **When you're really happy about something that someone has done, how do you tell that person?**

Say: **The people were so happy to see Jesus coming into their city. They knew all about how he healed lots of people, so they made what we call today a parade.** Have children form two parallel lines facing each other. Make sure the lines are about five

feet apart. The lines should be wide enough that children can ride their donkeys through with ease.

As Jesus and his friends entered the city, all the people were lining the streets, waving palm leaves. Give each child a palm frond. Place one of the children's favorite praise songs in a CD player, and let the children take turns riding their donkeys one at a time through the center of the lines as the other children wave their palm fronds. Pause the CD after a few minutes.

All the people were celebrating, "Hosanna, hosanna, the King of glory has come!" Play the CD again. Continue letting a few more children ride through the crowd on their donkeys. Have the rest of the crowd shout, "Hosanna!" and wave the palm fronds as they pretend Jesus is riding through. Then pause the CD.

Ask: • **What would you shout if Jesus were riding by?**

Say: **There were some people in the crowd who didn't want Jesus to be known, so they tried to stop the people from celebrating Jesus as King. They wanted the rest of the people to stop praising Jesus.** Have children turn to someone next to them, put their fingers over their mouths and say, "Shhhh."

But Jesus told his disciples about the mean people, because the people who were glad to see Jesus needed to cheer for him. They had been waiting for Jesus to come and be their King for many years. Play the CD one last time, and let children ride their donkeys through the crowd, wave their palm fronds, and shout, "Hosanna! Hosanna! Hosanna to the King!"

Ask: • **What has Jesus done that makes you excited?**

• **Who can you tell about Jesus?**

Children love to shout and cheer. Make sure they know that their cheers are to praise God, not just to make noise.

Jesus Washes the Disciples' Feet

Do You Want to Be First?

cd2 track 31

Sing "Do You Want to Be First?" to the tune of "Do Your Ears Hang Low?"

Jesus washed their feet (*pretend to wash feet*)
When he sat them down to eat. (*Pretend to eat.*)
Showed them how to help others (*hold hands, out, palms up*),
Both their sisters and their brothers. (*Point to a girl and a boy.*)

He wanted them to learn this. (*Hold out one hand, then the other.*)
It's a lesson not to miss. (*Shake index finger side to side.*)
Jesus washed their feet. (*Point up, then pretend to wash feet.*)

Do you want to be first? (*Hold up index finger.*)
Do you want to be the best? (*Flex biceps.*)
Then be willing to help others (*hold hands out, palms up*),
Both your sisters and your brothers. (*Point to a girl and a boy.*)

Just do it as he showed us (*hold out one hand, then the other*),
And help without a fuss. (*Shake index finger from side to side.*)
Then you can be first. (*Hold index finger above head.*)

I Help My Friend

Use this finger play to emphasize that when we help each other, we are obeying what Jesus asked us to do.

I have one Lord. (*Hold up one finger.*)

I have two feet. (*Hold up two fingers.*)

I have one heart (*draw a heart on chest*);

Feel it beat. (*Place one hand on chest, and pat it with the opposite hand.*)

I have two hands (*hold hands out*)

To help my friend. (*Point to a friend.*)

I'll follow Jesus (*point up to heaven*)

Until the end. (*Hold hands out, palms up.*)

Jesus Washes the Disciples' Feet •

John 13:1-17

Bible Point: Jesus wants us to serve others.

Jesus showed his disciples by example that they were to serve each other as well as serve him. In washing their feet, he carried out the task that usually the lowliest of servants performed. This lesson will help you teach your children that none of us is better than the other. We can serve and honor one another, just as Jesus served the disciples.

Give each child a paper towel before beginning the Bible story, and invite children to sit in a circle on the floor in front of you.

Say: **Jesus and his friends were getting ready to have dinner. They had walked all day in sandals, and their feet were very dirty. There was usually a servant who would go around and wash everyone's feet, but the disciples didn't see anyone. They must have wondered who would wash their dirty feet before they sat down to eat their dinner.**

Ask: • **What would you do if your feet needed to be washed?**

Say: **The disciples just wouldn't think to wash their own feet. That was the job of a servant. Suddenly, they saw Jesus begin to wash one of the disciple's feet. They were surprised! Jesus was too important to get down on the ground and wash someone's feet! But he did.** Have children show you their surprised faces.

Peter told Jesus that he didn't want him to wash his feet. Jesus was the important master. He was the boss. The boss shouldn't be washing *their* feet. Bosses should have the servants wash their

feet because the boss or master was the most important person. Have children take their paper towels, hide them behind their backs, and shake their heads "no" to the people next to them.

Jesus then told Peter that he wanted to wash their feet so that when he was gone, they would remember to do kind things for each other as he had done.

Ask: • **What are some kind things Jesus did?**

• **What are some kind things you can do for others?**

Say: **Jesus was an important person, but he cared about his disciples so much that he didn't care about his own importance. Jesus got down on the ground and washed all of his disciples' feet. Jesus wanted them to know that serving others and being kind make you important to God. Let's practice being important to God and clean each other's shoes. Jesus wants us to serve others.**

Help the children turn to a friend sitting next to them to form pairs. Have them sit facing each other with feet outstretched so that they can reach their partners' feet. Show your children how to rub the paper towels across their partners' shoes, pretending to clean them. Remind children that Jesus wants us to serve others.

It is not necessary for the children to take their shoes and socks off for this lesson. They can just wipe off each other's shoes.

Jesus Tells the Disciples to Remember Him

I'll Remember

cd2 track 32

Sing "I'll Remember" to the tune of "Jesus Loves Me."

Jesus said, "Remember me." *(Tap side of head.)*
Then he died for you and me. *(Spread arms wide.)*
I know Jesus is God's Son. *(Point up.)*
I'll remember what he's done. *(Hug yourself.)*

Yes, I'll remember. *(Tap side of head.)*
Yes, I'll remember.
Yes, I'll remember
That Jesus died for me. *(Spread arms wide.)*

Jesus is alive today. *(Point up.)*
He rose again on the third day. *(Squat and then rise, extending arms up.)*
He watches me from heaven above. *(Shield eyes with hand and look around.)*
I'll remember his great love. *(Hug yourself.)*

Yes, I'll remember. *(Tap side of head.)*
Yes, I'll remember.
Yes, I'll remember
That Jesus is alive. *(Spread arms wide.)*

Remembering Jesus

There are many things that can remind us of Jesus and how much he loves us. This finger play will help your children learn that they can think about Jesus wherever they are and whatever they are doing.

I remember Jesus when I sit under a tree. *(Put arms in a circle above head.)*

I remember Jesus 'cause he died for me.
(Spread arms out wide.)

I remember Jesus when I run and play. *(Run fingers up arm.)*

I remember Jesus 'cause he's with me every day. *(Hug yourself.)*

Jesus Tells the Disciples to Remember Him

Luke 22:7-20

Bible Point: Jesus wants us to remember him.

Jesus was a master teacher and knew that we remember things better when we see, hear, and touch real objects. By using the bread and the cup, items we use every day, Jesus was assured that we would remember him and the sacrifice he made so that we might have eternal life. When sharing this lesson with your children, remember that you are one of the first people in their lives to help them remember who Jesus is.

Before you begin, bring in a few pictures of common objects or symbols, such as a Christmas tree, an Easter egg, signal lights, or a moon. You'll also need a wrapped loaf of bread.

The children will have fun remembering special people and time with you. As you read the story, let the children share their experiences with you.

Ask: • **What does each of these pictures remind you of?**

Hold up your pictures, one at a time, allowing children to share their memories.

Say: **These things remind me of special times too. It's fun to remember things and especially people who are special to us.**

Ask: • **What special person can you remember?**

• **What do you remember about that person?**

Say: **Jesus knew that he would be going away, so he wanted his disciples to remember him when he was gone. Jesus picked up some bread from the table and told his disciples to remember him every time they saw and took a piece of bread to eat. Jesus told his disciples that the bread was like a** symbol, or reminder, of his body that hung on the cross for all the bad things we do.

Pass around the loaf of bread. As each child holds the bread, have him or her answer the following question:

Ask: • **What's one thing you can remember about Jesus?**

Say: **While the disciples were eating, Jesus picked up his cup and told his disciples to remember him every time they drank their juice. Jesus told his disciples that the juice was like his blood that was given so we could be forgiven.**

Ask: • **What do you want Jesus to forgive you of?**

Say: **Because Jesus died on the cross, God can now forgive us for all the bad things we have done.**

Jesus Came to Die for Us

That's Why He Died

cd2 track 33

Sing "That's Why He Died" to the tune of "Jesus Loves Me."

On a cross my Jesus died. *(Spread arms out wide.)*

His disciples stood and cried *(pretend to cry and rub eyes)*

Because they could not understand

That this was part of God's good plan. *(Point up.)*

Chorus:

Yes, Jesus loves me. *(Make sign for "Jesus," hug yourself, then point to yourself.)*

Yes, Jesus loves me.

Yes, Jesus loves me.

That's why he died for me. *(Spread arms out wide.)*

Jesus gave his life that day *(spread arms out wide)*

So he could take my sins away. *(Pretend to erase bad things from heart.)*

Now I'll live as God's true friend. *(Hug yourself.)*

In heaven my life will never end. *(Point up, then wag finger.)*

(Repeat chorus.)

Jesus' Love

Before beginning, explain to your children that "Calvary's tree" means the cross where Jesus died and that God's forgiveness is like erasing the bad things that we do.

Jesus loves you *(point to a friend),*

And Jesus loves me. *(Point to yourself.)*

He showed us his love *(hug yourself)*

On Calvary's tree. *(Spread arms out wide.)*

Forgiving our sins *(pretend to erase bad things from heart),*

That's why he died *(spread arms out wide)—*

So we can be in heaven *(point up to heaven)*

Forever by his side. *(Raise and shake hands above head.)*

Jesus Came to Die for Us

Luke 22:39–23:56

Bible Point: Jesus loves us, so he died for our sins.

Before class, create four paper crosses for each child. Invite your children to sit with you on the floor. Open your Bible to Luke 22, and show the children the words. As you read the following Bible story, have children use markers, crayons, and glitter to decorate their crosses at the appropriate time.

Say: **Jesus came to earth many years ago as a baby. Then he grew up and became a man. Jesus was to die on a cross so that our sins could be forgiven and we could live in heaven with him forever. Let's find out how that happened.**

Many people saw the miracles that Jesus did and saw how he healed those who were sick. They listened to what he taught them about God, and they loved him.

There were some people who hated Jesus. They told other people that Jesus was lying when he said he was God's Son. They wouldn't believe that people were really healed. They were mad because Jesus claimed to forgive people's sins (the bad things they did). The more famous Jesus became, the angrier these people got. They decided to look for a way to get rid of Jesus forever.

Have each child decorate one cross to show the people who were mad at Jesus. For example, children can draw sad faces, mad faces, or angry people.

Say: **Jesus knew that these men didn't like him and were planning to kill him, but he trusted God's plan. Jesus knew that God loved him and all the people on earth. Jesus knew that he had to die so that our sins could be forgiven forever. Jesus was willing to do the hardest thing because he loves us that much!**

One night Jesus took his disciples to a quiet garden to pray. While Jesus was praying, the bad men came with lots of soldiers, arrested Jesus, and took him to jail.

When the disciples saw Jesus arrested and taken to jail, they were afraid. They wondered if they would be arrested and taken to jail, too, so they ran away. Have each child decorate one cross to demonstrate Jesus' arrest. For example, children can draw frightened faces, soldiers, or Jesus praying.

The soldiers and the bad men were very mean to Jesus and hurt him. They said mean things to him and told him he was lying when he was really telling the truth. Jesus had never done anything bad in his whole life, and these mean people were being very unfair to him. But Jesus knew that this was God's plan. Jesus knew that he had to die on a cross so that our sins could be forgiven forever. Jesus was willing to do the hardest thing because he loves us that much!

They brought Jesus and another bad man who was also in jail before a crowd of people and asked the people which one they should put on a cross to die.

Ask: • **Who do you think they chose?**

Say: **The crowd of people turned against Jesus and said that Jesus should die on the cross. How** *unfair*! **Jesus was** *innocent*; **he hadn't done** *anything* **wrong! But Jesus knew that this was God's plan. Jesus knew that he had to die on a cross so that our sins could be forgiven forever. Jesus was willing to do the hardest thing because he loves us that much!**

Have each child decorate one cross to demonstrate the crucifixion. For example, children could draw tears or Jesus on the cross.

Say: **This made Jesus' friends very sad. Show me what your face would look like if you were very sad for Jesus.** Let children show you sad faces. **Jesus told his friends not to be sad. Jesus knew that this was God's plan. Jesus knew that he needed to die so that God could forgive our sins. That was the only way we could all live forever in heaven with him. Jesus was willing to do the hardest thing because he loves us that much!**

Jesus' friends, the disciples, cried for three days. But at the end of those three days, something very miraculous happened that no one expected. God brought Jesus back to life! God's plan was perfect! Jesus was alive! Our sins could now be forgiven, and we can live forever with him in heaven. That's how much Jesus loves us!

Have each child decorate one cross to demonstrate the Resurrection. For example, children could draw smiles, Jesus in a white robe, or an empty tomb.

This is a good time to ask children if they would like Jesus to forgive their sins (the bad things they've done). End with the following prayer:

Dear God, thank you for loving us so much that you let Jesus die on a cross for our sins. Please forgive the bad things we've done. We love you. In Jesus' name, amen.

God Sends His Holy Spirit

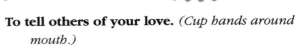
cd2 track 34

Blow, Blow, Blow the Wind

Sing "Blow, Blow, Blow the Wind" to the tune of "Row, Row, Row Your Boat."

Blow, blow, blow the wind. *(Blow gently.)*
Blow strong if you can. *(Blow hard.)*

God sent us the Holy Spirit
Like a mighty wind. *(Blow as hard as you can.)*

God Sends His Holy Spirit

Holy Spirit come to me. *(Motion to come.)*

Holy Spirit set me free *(swing arms out wide)*

To tell others of your love. *(Cup hands around mouth.)*

Holy Spirit from above. *(Raise hands, palms up.)*

God Sends His Holy Spirit

Acts 2:1-21; 3:12-19

Bible Point: The Holy Spirit is our helper.

Before you begin, cut crepe paper streamers in yellow, orange, and red about eight to ten inches long. You'll need one of each color for each of your children. Tape the three pieces together at one end so that the children can hold them.

Invite your children to join you in sitting down on the floor. Open your Bible to Acts 2, and show children the words.

Say: **Just before Jesus went back to heaven, he promised his friends, the disciples, that he would send a helper for them. That helper was called the Holy Spirit. Jesus knew that the disciples were going to need help being brave enough to tell others about Jesus. So Jesus promised them the Holy Spirit if they waited and prayed.**

Ask: • **Have you ever needed help to be brave? When?**

• **Have you ever told anyone something about God or Jesus? What did you tell that person?**

Say: **The disciples obeyed Jesus and waited and prayed. When all of the disciples were praying together during a holiday called Pentecost, God did something very special.** Give children the crepe paper flames you made. Tell them to be ready to wave them

during the Bible story.

Ask: • **What are some things you like to do when you celebrate something special, like a birthday or holiday?**

Say: **The disciples had good food to eat, and they were praising God. Suddenly, God sent his helper, the Holy Spirit. First the wind began to blow. Let's blow like the wind. Whooooo! Whooooo!** Lead children in blowing on one another.

Then there were flames of fire dancing above their heads. Let's make pretend fire with our colored streamers. Can you dance and twirl around and make the fire all around you?

Blow the wind with your mouth, and twirl around with your fire streamers. Jesus sent the Holy Spirit for us!

Let's set our fire streamers down, sit down in a circle, and hold hands.

In the Bible story, everyone was praying at the same time in different languages, and God heard all of their prayers. So let's close our eyes, and I want you to think of one way you need God's help today. Then when I say, "Dear God," I want all of you to talk out loud at the same time and tell God one way you need his help.

Dear God...

Amen.

Because the Holy Spirit is our helper and God's helper, he helped God to hear all of our prayers right then. And the Holy Spirit will help you with whatever you need.

An Angel Frees Peter From Jail

Peter's Free

cd12 track 35

Help the children form groups of three or four. Choose two of the four children to create a bridge as in the game London Bridge. Have the third child stand in between the two children that are creating the bridge. Have the children creating the bridge bring their arms down during the song so that the third child is locked in the center as you sing the verses. Lead your children in singing "Peter's Free" to the tune of "The Mulberry Bush."

Lock Peter up and hold him tight (*bring arms down and "lock" child in the center*),
Hold him tight (*rock center child back and forth gently*),
Hold him tight.
Lock Peter up and hold him tight.
Don't let him out of jail.

These chains will never stay on him (*rock center child back and forth gently*),
Stay on him,
Stay on him.
These chains will never stay on him
'Cause God will set him free! (*Open arms.*)

An Angel Frees Peter From Jail

Have fun acting this out and building confidence in your children that God answers prayer.

Peter, Peter, he's in jail. (*Place open fingers in front of face like jail bars.*)
I'm sure he wants to cry and wail. (*Pretend to rub eyes as if crying.*)
Moms and dads, sisters and brothers
Are praying to their heavenly Father. (*Make praying hands.*)

An angel appeared at Peter's side. (*Make a circle with hands on top of head, like a halo.*)
The doors of the jail swung open wide. (*Put hands together in front of you, then spread them out like gates opening.*)
Peter knocked on the door where his friends did stay. (*Use fist to knock on an imaginary door.*)
They all shouted, "God answers us when we pray!" (*Put hands up high, then in prayer position.*)

The Angel Frees Peter From Jail

Acts 12:1-18

Bible Point: God wants us to pray for others.

Use this story to help children learn that God wants us to pray for others.

This story can be told without props, but here are some suggested props to add interest to the story: child's bathrobe for Peter, two covered stretchy hair bands for the prison guards, and an aluminum-foil halo or white choir robe for the angel.

Before you begin, select one child to be Peter, two more children to be the jail guards, one child to be the angel, and one child to answer the door when "Peter" knocks. Tell children the titles of their roles, and ask them to listen carefully for when they will act out their parts within the story. Tell the other children that they will have some actions during the Bible story. Tell the story with your back to the door of the room and near the light switch, if possible. Begin this story with the lights out. If you have children who are afraid of the dark, dim the lights, if possible, or leave the door ajar.

Say: **In the book of Acts in our Bible, there is a story about an amazing way God answered the prayers of his people for a man named Peter. Here's Peter now.** Have "Peter" come and sit next to you, facing the children.

Peter was a man who loved Jesus and talked about him wherever he went. Some people didn't like Peter talking about Jesus, so they put him in jail. Have the two jailers come and sit on either side of Peter. Use the hair bands to connect Peter's wrists to a wrist of each jailer as if they were chains or handcuffs.

In Bible times when people were put in jail, they were connected to each other with chains. Let's all pretend we're in jail with Peter and hold hands with the people next to us.

While Peter was in jail, his friends were all praying together, asking God to get Peter out of jail. There might have been dads, moms, grandparents, and kids praying together. Keep holding hands, and let's pretend to pray for Peter like his friends did. Dear God, please help Peter get out of jail. We need

him to help us tell everyone about Jesus. Amen.

Suddenly there was a bright light in the jail. Turn on the lights. **An angel came to the jail and stood next to Peter. The chains fell off, and the guards didn't even wake up!** Have the angel remove the hair bands from Peter's wrists.

Ask: • **What do you think the angel might have said to Peter?**

Have Peter and the angel go outside the door of your classroom, wait for a moment, and then knock to come in.

Say: **Do you remember what Peter's friends were doing while he was in jail? Let's pretend to be those friends again and pretend to pray for Peter. Someone is knocking.** Send a child to open the door. **Look! It's Peter! God has answered our prayers! Peter is out of prison and ready to help us tell others about Jesus.**

Ask: • **How would you feel if you saw Peter standing at your door?**

• **How do you think Peter felt being out of jail?**

• **How has God answered your prayers?**

Say: **God doesn't always answer our prayers the way we want him to, but we can remember to always pray for others. God answers prayers when we pray the way he wants us to pray.**

The children acting certain parts will need some coaching from you along the way. Just whisper the needed coaching to a child and then continue telling the Bible story in a louder voice. Preschool children won't even notice the slight interruption to the story.

Lydia Is Converted

The Good News

track 36 cd12

Sing "The Good News" to the tune of "The B-I-B-L-E."

Tell about the good news. (*Put hands together like a book.*)
Tell about God's Word.
Tell about the good news
So Jesus can be heard. (*Point up.*)

Jesus came to save us.
Jesus came to die. (*Spread arms out wide.*)

Jesus came to save us all;
On him you can rely. (*Lean on a friend.*)

Tell about the good news. (*Put hands together like a book.*)
Tell about God's Word.
Tell about the good news
So Jesus can be heard. (*Point up.*)

Lydia Is Converted

As you lead your children in this finger play, remind them that God wants us to tell everyone about Jesus.

Doctors, teachers, officers tall (*point at imaginary people*)

Need to hear of Jesus' love. (*Hug yourself.*)

Asians, Africans, Americans all (*point at imaginary people*)

Need to know of God above. (*Hold hands up toward the sky.*)

Boys and girls, both young and old (*pat the air as if patting little heads*),

Need to hear God's story told. (*Cup hands around ears.*)

Lydia Is Converted

Acts 16:9-15

Bible Point: God wants us to tell everyone about Jesus.

Paul, Silas, and probably Timothy traveled to spend some time with people who loved God. One day they were gathering near the river for prayer. A woman named Lydia was an important businesswoman in the city and a worshipper of God, too. Lydia heard the message about Jesus and gave her life to the Lord. She and her whole household were baptized in the river. As you talk about this story with the children, emphasize that they can tell anyone about Jesus.

Before you begin, use crepe paper, a long piece of blue cloth, bulletin board paper, or a sheet to create a river on the classroom floor. Encourage the children to gather near the "river."

Separate the children into three groups. Tell one group that they are the River group and they are to wiggle their fingers and move their hands across the front of them like a flowing river every time they hear the word *river* in the story. Tell the second group that they are the Ears group. They are to cup their ears with their hands every time they hear the word *ears* in the story. Tell the third group that they are the Heart group and they are to draw heart outlines on their chests each time they hear the word *heart* in the story. Now have the three groups gather and sit on the edge of the river.

Say: **Paul was a man who loved God with all his** *heart*. Pause for kids to respond. **He traveled with Timothy and Silas and others who loved God with all of their** *hearts* (pause for kids to respond) **and used their** *ears* (pause for kids to respond) **to listen to God's Word. They traveled from town to town to tell people about Jesus and to trust him with their whole** *hearts*. Pause for kids to respond.

One day Paul and his friends were walking near a *river* (pause for kids to respond) **and found a group of women who gathered there to pray. Paul and his friends sat down and began to tell the women about Jesus. One of the women who was listening with her** *ears* (pause for kids to respond) **was named Lydia. She sold purple cloth and was an important person in her city. She believed in God, but she had never heard about Jesus. After she listened with her** *ears* (pause for kids to respond) **to the message Paul and his friends told about Jesus,** the Lord opened her *heart* (pause for kids to respond) **to respond to Paul's message.**

She and her whole family gave their *hearts* (pause for kids to respond) **to Jesus that day. It was so good that Lydia had not only just gathered with God's people and listened with her** *ears* (pause for kids to respond), **but she also had responded to the Lord with her** *heart*. Pause for kids to respond. **Everyone who lived in her house was baptized that day in the** *river*. Pause for kids to respond. **Lydia was so excited that she invited the men to stay at her house and said she would take care of them every time they came to her city.**

You'll want to emphasize the italicized words to help cue the children to do their motions at the right times during the story.

Paul and Silas Go to Jail

Jailer Jingle

Sing "Jailer Jingle" to the turn of "The Battle Hymn of the Republic." Children will sing the chorus.

Paul and Silas told about the coming of the Lord. (*Point up.*)

They were thrown in jail, and they were locked up to a board.

The jailer watched them carefully and showed them his sharp sword. (*Pretend to hold up a sword.*)

How can these men be saved?

Chorus:

Jesus, Jesus, Jesus saves us. (*Point up, then open arms wide like a cross.*)

Jesus, Jesus, Jesus saves us. (*Repeat motions.*)

Jesus, Jesus, Jesus saves us. (*Repeat motions.*)

Believe and you'll be saved! (*Hug yourself.*)

Paul and Silas were in jail, but still they sang throughout the night. (*Wave hands as if conducting a choir.*)

They knew that God was watching, so they didn't feel a fright. (*Point up.*)

They trusted God to help them, so they didn't even fight.

They knew that Jesus saves. (*Hug yourself.*)

(Repeat chorus.)

The earth began to tremble, and the jail began to shake. (*Shake body.*)

God had sent a super, mighty, five-point-O earthquake.

The prison doors flew open, and their chains began to break! (*Pretend to open doors.*)

God had set them free! (*Throw arms out wide.*)

(Repeat chorus.)

The jailer rushed inside then, and he knelt in front of Paul. (*Kneel down.*)

"Tell me, how can I be saved and on whose name should I now call?"

Paul and Silas told him that the Lord Christ saves us all. (*Point up.*)

Believe and you'll be saved!

(Repeat chorus.)

Jesus Saves Us

As you teach children this rhyme, remind them that Jesus saves us.

Because of the wrong things I sometimes do (*give thumbs down*),

I need Jesus to help me through. (*Put arms around a friend's shoulders.*)

Because of what Jesus did on the cross (*spread arms wide*),

I can live in heaven free of cost. (*Point up.*)

I love Jesus! He listens to me! *(Cup hands around ears.)*

He loves me, and he sets me free! *(Hug yourself.)*

Paul and Silas Go to Jail

Acts 16:16-34

Bible Point: We can praise God when things are bad.

Paul and Silas were unfairly arrested and put in jail. They could have complained, saying, "It's not fair," but instead they seized the opportunity to set a Christian example wherever they were. Use this story to show your children that they can trust God no matter where they are.

Direct the children to sit in a circle on the floor.

Say: **Paul and Silas were two men who loved Jesus very much. They were walking everywhere they could and telling people about Jesus.** Direct children to remain seated but move their feet as if walking. **But there were some people who got really mad when God used Paul and Silas to make people better. One day some of the people got so mad that they had Paul and Silas arrested and thrown in jail.** Select two children to pretend to be Paul and Silas and sit inside the circle. **Their feet were put in chains.** Choose two other children to be the jailers and pretend to attach chains to Paul's and Silas' feet.

Ask: • **How would you feel if you were in jail and your feet were in chains?**

• **Do you think you could sing and praise God? Why or why not?**

Say: **Paul and Silas trusted God to take care of them, so they began to pray and sing.**

Let's all pretend we are Paul and Silas in jail and sing a song of praise to God.

Lead your children in singing "Worship God" (words found on page 122) on your CD.

Say: **While Paul and Silas were singing, an earthquake started making the earth shake and tremble. Help me make an earthquake.** Have children make fists and pound the floor in front of them to make a loud rumble.

When the earthquake was over, the jail doors opened, and the chains fell off Paul and Silas. They were free, but they didn't run away. Have the children in the middle of the circle come back and join the larger circle.

The man in charge of watching the prisoners came running over. He was sure the prisoners had gotten away and was so surprised to find them sitting there.

Ask: • **How would you feel if there was an earthquake?**

• **Would you run out of the jail? Why or why not?**

Say: **The jailer realized that they loved Jesus and that Jesus had saved them. The jailer asked how he could know and love Jesus too. His whole family was baptized, and they had a party to celebrate.**

Let's celebrate by singing our song again. You can jump and dance and celebrate while we sing the song. If you have streamers or musical instruments, let the children take turns playing them during the song.

Paul Is Shipwrecked

Scared, Scared

track 38

Sing "Scared, Scared" to the tune of "Row, Row, Row Your Boat."

Scared, scared, scared we are *(show scared face)*
On the stormy sea. *(Make wave motions.)*

God told me that we would be
Safe, he guaranteed. *(Hug yourself.)*

You Can Do It!

Your children will delight in saying and doing the motions to this finger play as they encourage those around them.

"You can do it!" I will say *(cup hands around mouth)*

To help my friends at work or play. *(Clap hands.)*

"Way to go!" is what I'll shout. *(Show two thumbs up.)*

That is what it's all about.

Paul Is Shipwrecked

Acts 27

Bible Point: God wants us to encourage others.

In this Bible story, we find Paul aboard a ship of prisoners. He has had a message from God, which he shares with the ship's captain, warning about an upcoming storm. The captain chooses not to heed the warning, and the ship and its passengers are in a severe storm for fourteen days. Paul receives another message from God promising that all will survive the storm. Use this story to build children's confidence that, even though there are storms in our lives, God will take care of us. We can encourage others when things are bad.

Before you begin, use masking tape to mark the outline of a ship on the floor. Make it large enough for your children to sit inside during the Bible story.

Say: **Paul was a man who had risked his life to tell others about Jesus. He was traveling on a ship and talking to God. God told him that there was a storm coming. He went to find the captain of the boat to tell him that they probably shouldn't sail right then, but the captain wouldn't listen to Paul. So the ship sailed out to sea, even though the captain had been warned.**

Let's pretend we are in that ship and have to row. Show children how to put their arms out in front of themselves and pretend to row. **This is a big ship with lots of people, so we have to work really hard.** Pretend to row harder.

There are clouds in the sky. Point up to the sky. **It's starting to rain.** Wiggle your fingers and move your arms up and down to make pretend rain. **The wind is blowing.** Blow air from your mouth. **We better row faster and harder to try to get out of this storm.** Pretend to row faster.

The storm kept coming. It rained more and more. Wiggle your fingers and move your arms up and down to make pretend rain. **Even the sailors were starting to get scared now.**

Ask: • **How would you feel if you were in a bad storm?**

• **What might you say to the friend next to you so that he or she wouldn't feel as afraid?**

Say: **Well, the wind kept blowing.** Blow air. **Uh-oh! Some water is getting into the boat.**

Ask: • **What do you think the people on the boat should do?**

Say: **We better scoop out the water. Let's cup our hands and pretend to scoop out the water and throw it back into the ocean.**

The storm lasted for fourteen days. Let's count all those days. Count to fourteen. **Every day the men on the boat got more and more afraid. Paul knew that God wants us to encourage others, so he said nice things to all the men.**

Ask: • **What's something nice that you might say to someone to help him or her feel better?**

Say: **The men on the ship thought they would all die in the storm, but Paul encouraged them so that they would feel better. Paul told the men that they should have listened to him. But God also sent an angel who told Paul that they didn't need to be afraid because no one would die in the storm. God told Paul that the ship would get wrecked in the storm but that everyone would be safe. When Paul encouraged them, they felt better.**

Soon they could see dry land and turned the ship to go that way. Have children all lean one direction in the "boat." **But the ship got stuck in the ground at the bottom of the sea and broke into pieces. The men had to climb out and swim to shore.** Have children pretend to swim to shore. **Just as God had promised, no one was hurt, and they were all on dry land together. Paul was right.**

Direct children to climb out of the boat now that they're safely on shore and sit down.

Say: **Paul gave them some food to eat and led them in a prayer of thanksgiving to God for keeping his promise that he would take care of them. God wants us to encourage others, just as Paul encouraged the other men on the boat when they were scared.**

Ask: • **What are some ways you can encourage your friends or family when they're having a hard day?**

Give children some fish-shaped crackers. While the kids are eating, talk about the storm in the Bible story and the times in kids' lives when they might feel afraid. Remind children that God always takes care of us and he wants us to encourage others, too.

Money, Money

Scripture Index